Wake Up Your Writing

with the TRICKS of the Old Pros

The Literary and Rhetorical Devices of the Ancient Greeks and Romans

Frank Gerace, Ph.D.

DEDICATION

I dedicate this book to all my teachers who instilled in me a love of language. I also thank my students at LaGuardia

Community College in Long Island City, N.Y. who with their questions and desire to learn have pushed me to be clearer and clearer in my explanations.

My friend and guide Juan Tapia in Bolivia drilled me in Quechua to get me to feel a language without needing to know the grammar. My friend and fellow exile in Peru, Fidencio Hernando Lázaro taught me that when you have something to say, you have to just sit down and write it. That advice was the motivation for my first Book, *Comunicación Horizontal: Ascenso de Masas y Movilización Social.*

I also dedicate it to my grandchildren. I hope they treasure the legacy of learning that I leave them. Finally, I thank my loving wife, Miriam, for her support and patience as this book came together.

ACKNOWLEDGEMENTS

I acknowledge the use of many resources gathered over the years for my classes at La Guardia Community College in Long Island City, New York. I have tried to make this material and the results of other research my own by adapting it to my needs and chosen format. If I have failed in this task, I apologize and am committed to immediately correct any errors or misattributions.

THANKS to:

My friends and family who have put up with my corny puns for years. I also thank them in advance for what they will have to put up with as I begin to use rhetorical devices in my breakfast table conversations.

Introduction

You want to be able to write English. This is great! If you want it, you will get it. The fact that you are reading this book means that you are committed to learning to write English better.

I know people who learned English as adults and speak it very well but who feel they cannot write anything in English. They are afraid of their grammar, usage, and spelling. But even people who are almost perfect in the language will make mistakes; therefore it is foolish for weaker writers to be afraid of making mistakes. It is a shame that because of their holding back they lose the benefits of writing.

You can get help from teachers, from books, and even from apps on your phone. But most crucial is the practice you put in.

One thing you can do is to copy good writing of whatever kind interests you, letters, business writing, literature, etc. But there is so much writing around; what should you concentrate on?

Here's an idea. You can't go wrong by learning the writing strategies that have been around for thousands of years.

1

These "tricks" come from what are called "rhetorical devices". You'll see them in this book.

Rhetoric is the art of speaking and writing with the goal of helping speakers or writers to inform, explain, praise, attack, persuade, or achieve other goals of their communication.

Rhetoric has been studied and practiced in the Western world for thousands of years. In the 4th century BC Aristotle called it *"the faculty of observing in any given case the available means of persuasion."* Scholars in classical Rome taught that rhetoric helps the writer to find, organize, and beautify his or her thoughts, as well as aiding with the memory and delivery of the content.

The editors of the King James Bible were steeped in classical literature. Their influences show in the many examples of the use of rhetorical devices in the Bible that are included in this book. Their work shows us the place of the Rhetorical Devices in good writing where we can call them Literary Devices.

You want to be able to write better. One way to good writing is through reading. Recognizing a few rhetorical devices in your reading will be a satisfaction to you.

Hopefully, seeing these tools in action will prompt you to use them. If you do, you will express yourself better as you craft the connections between the way you write and what you write.

Literary/rhetorical devices are not just blasts from the past; today's writers use them also. They use them so well, they must have studied them. For example, Martin Luther King, Jr. in 1958 in his *Stride Toward Freedom: The Montgomery Story* used the classical device called Climax or Gradation. This writer's tool is the arranging of words or sentences according to increasing importance, weight, or emphasis.
Look at MLK's use of this:

> *Men often hate each other because they fear each other; they fear each other because they don't know each other; they don't know each other because they can not communicate; they can not communicate because they are separated.*

The literary/rhetorical devices presented in the rest of this book generally fall into three general categories:

1. Emphasis and Clarification
2. Organization and Arrangement
3. Style and Display

The "tricks" presented in this book are grouped into these categories to make their interrelationships clear to you.

This will also help you remember the differences among them so you can search for the appropriate device as you are writing.

And just for fun, for you to show off at barbecues and cocktail parties, we give you their names in Greek.

There are many speaking and writing strategies within the above general classes. You will have to sample and experiment before you get to feel comfortable with these devices, but don't practice too much in a single piece of work. Practice in a "minor league" notebook. When the tools become familiar to you, and when it no longer feels forced or false to use them, when they get to be part of your writing style and not just added on, then they can make it to the "major leagues" and be used in an article or other real piece of your writing.

You don't have to use a lot of these devices to be a good writer. Actually, if you use them too much or carelessly, they will make your work weaker not stronger. But with a little care and skill, and a lot of practice, you will write with more power and impact.

Remember that the aids to writing have to do with:

- *stressing or clarifying your thoughts*;

- other aids will help you
  organize, and arrange your content;

- and there are others more involved with the *style and attractiveness of your writing.*

Practice them; try them out. Don't worry if they ring false at first. Play with them; learn to manipulate and control your words and ideas and even the reader's mind, answering their queries, helping them compare and balance alternatives.

Sometimes a given device will fit best in only one category, but often any one device has multiple characteristics and can fit in more than one category.

There are many literary and rhetorical devices. This little book will present only a few of them. Learn them; use them little by little. You will find a few of the most useful ones in the following pages.

Now, after encouraging you to use rhetorical devices, it is necessary to say that the success of a figure of speech and of all rhetorical devices depends on the reader or hearer. Be careful! Don't go over their head.

CONTENTS Chapter One: P. 9

EMPHASIS AND CLARIFICATION

CONTENTS Chapter Two: P.58

ORGANIZATION AND ARRANGEMENT

CONTENTS Chapter Three: P. 96

STYLE AND DISPLAY

Chapter One:

Emphasis and Clarification

There are many devices that add impact to your writing. One example is one that repeats the same word or phrase with no other word in between.

> *Never give in, never, never, never, never, in nothing great or small, large or petty, never give in except to convictions of honour and good sense. Never yield to force.*
> **Winston Churchill.**

Supersize it!

The Romans called this Amplificatio

In the world of words the word "amplification" does not mean to make bigger, but rather to provide more ample information. By the way, did you notice how in the previous sentence we *distinguished*, as called for by the device *distinctio* on page 33

Sometimes you will want to call attention to, emphasize, and expand a word or idea to make sure the reader realizes the relevance or centrality that you give it in the discussion.

You can amplify the meaning of a word or expression by adding more detail to it. In this way you emphasize what might otherwise be passed over.

>*The basis of a democracy is its citizens, active, involved, and concerned defenders of their rights.*

>*My old neighborhood, not exclusive, but crowded, noisy, full of friends, fills my memories.*

Sometimes more than words are added to the description; there may be entire phrases.

>*Once in a poor country, I visited the*

abandoned house of an ex-president. The house had been destroyed during a revolution against the class that he represented.

Despite the intervening years, we could get a feel for the opulence of his living by careful observation of faint hints: the silk wall paper in a land of mud walls, the variety and quality of the glazed roof tiles in a land of palm thatch roofs, broken china in a land of gourd bowls.

The mailman does his job, walking through rain, snow, smog, barking dogs, garbage in the streets, just to bring us unwanted junk mail.

This summer's movies were bad, and some of them very bad, but the one I just saw was absolutely horrible.

Corruption, rampant corruption is the bane of our politics.

He had expensive tastes, a taste for good wine, good food, and hand tailored clothes.

The device of amplification can overlap with or include repetition when the repeated word adds further definition or detail. Repetition with added detail is more powerful than plain, "straight" syntax.

In the following pairs of expressions, observe how the second expressions, which repeats the key words "time" and "afraid", are stronger.

> *In everything remember the passing of a time which cannot be called again.*

> *In everything remember the passing of time, a time which cannot be called again.*

> *Be very afraid.*

> *Be afraid, very afraid.*

Remember, the Romans called this Amplificatio.

___

Eat more fish — politics is a dirty game
The Greeks called this Anacoluthon

Breaking off a thought and finishing a sentence with a different grammatical structure than that you begin with was an artifice used by the Greeks to gain attention. It is a grammatical interruption or lack of implied sequence within a sentence.

In other words, writers who use this powerful device begin a sentence in a way that aims at a certain logical result, but conclude it differently from what is expected.

This can be either an error of grammar or a stylistic virtue, depending on its use. In either case, it is an interruption or a fault of grammatical symmetry. We do this a lot when we speak or 'talk to ourselves" in our interior thought, so it suggests such personal thought when we use it in writing.
Itis often employed either to imitate ungrammatical, confused and informal speech or to draw the attention of readers.

Anacoluthon is used a lot in poetry, plays and dramatic monologues. This technique is well-suited to the loose, unorganized "stream of consciousness" writing which presents a character's thoughts next to one another, because the thoughts are sometimes inconsistent and often grammatically incorrect.

13

Examples:

Be careful with this device because improperly used it can—well, I have cautioned you enough already.

"I will have such revenges on you both,
That all the world shall — I will do such things, What they are, yet I know not."
(William Shakespeare, King Lear)

Bankers, known for their white collar crimes — are they to be forgiven with just a slap on the wrist?

Remember that the Greek meaning is that the expression "does not follow". This can be as a result of real or fake emotion as in the examples above. To know and apply this trick correctly can help your writing.

Rimbaud and Verlaine, precious pair of poets, Genius in both (but what is genius?) playing Chess on a marble table at an inn...

Discussing, between moves, iamb and

spondee Anacoluthon and the open vowel

Conrad Aiken: *Preludes for Memnon*

However, to write expressions that do not follow is often a grammatical error that must be avoided. Some examples are:

I saw an eagle flying with my binoculars.

I shot a bear in my pajamas.

Remember, the Greeks called this Anacoluthon.

Next to you, he's an Einstein!
Analogy

An analogy is a comparison in which characteristics of one thing (a person, an idea, an action, or a thing) are compared to those of something else.

It makes more comparisons than a simile (page 159) or a metaphor (page 117) which only compare two things. An analogy may be <u>presented by</u> a simile or an analogy but also extends the comparison in some way.

> *Analogy plays a significant role in problem solving such as, decision making, perception, memory, creativity, emotion, explanation and communication. It lies behind basic tasks such as the identification of places, objects and people, for example, in face perception and facial recognition systems. It has been argued that analogy is "the core of cognition".* **Wikipedia**

To succeed as a writer you must master the use of analogies. They are a sign and an exercise of intelligence. Using them opens up to our readers an awareness of the depth of your concerns and leads you to more complex, more nuanced, clearer exposition of your thoughts.

They are equally useful to fiction as they are to non-fiction, even scientific writing.

They fascinate us so much that they are used in **popular sayings and jokes**. Sometimes they are explicit and other times part of the elements of the comparison are not stated, much as the case with the syllogism. (page 180)

>*Their friendship went from hot to cool.*

>*I dance like a Sumo wrestler with a wasp in his underwear.*

>*Arguing with her is as effective as pissing against the wind.*

>*To see Doctor Jones diagnose a patient's ills is to see a detective investigating a crime.*

>*A mouse's squeak is louder than her loudest shout.*

>*Mother's speed and effectiveness in her kitchen could be measured against any modern corporation's operation.*

Analogies are used in scientific reasoning.

>*Buoyancy is simply the density of a solid object relative to the fluid it is sitting in.*

The Brownian motion is very similar to where you have a dust particle and you put it in a fluid. As the atoms hit against this dust particle it starts to jostle around, and the fluctuations in the number of atoms that hit from the left and the right actually make the dust particle move.
Steven Chu, Nobel Prize Winner, 1997

Rutherford's model of the atom (modified by Niels Bohr) made an analogy between the atom and the solar system. **Wikipedia**

They are often used in "intelligence" tests and estimates of reasoning ability to gauge the candidate's grasp of comparisons in vocabulary, art, science, and math.

(x) is to SLAG as FIRE is to ASHES.
A. quarry, B. furnace, C. mill, D. silo

Writers use them heavily to get their points across in striking ways.

"... their hands (were) always on him in a careful, caressing grip, as though all the while feeling him to make sure he was there. It was like men handling a fish which is still alive and may jump back into the water."
George Orwell, A Hanging

"Writing a book of poetry is like dropping a rose petal down the Grand Canyon and waiting for the echo." **Don Marquis**

"The white mares of the moon rush along the sky beating their golden hoofs upon the glass Heavens."
Amy Lowell, Night Clouds.

Remember, The Greeks, the Romans and we all call this Analogy.

She's no fun but she's rich
The Greeks called this Antanagoge

A good writer can place a criticism and compliment together to lessen the impact - *The car is banged up but it gets great gas mileage.*

You can call this trick "putting a positive spin" on something that is negative or difficult. The aim of this device is to turn a negative view into a positive one,

If we must criticize another person, one way is to soften the blow by starting off with a positive comment. Or we can end with a positive thought, making a "sandwich" with positive comments before and after negative ones, or vice versa.

In your writing you can bring up a positive side of an issue to respond to the negative view of an adversary. However, you need to point to real or well-argued positive aspects of the issue or you will be accused of being superficial or Pollyanna.

The installation of the new irrigation is expensive but it will use less water and allow more efficient delivery to the plants.

The disgraced politician said he

20

hated to lose his job, but he was looking forward to spending more time with his family.

When life gives me a lemon, I make lemonade.

True, he always forgets our anniversary, but he takes me out to eat.

Our products may cost more than those of the competition but they last much longer.

It is hard for a child to realize that their parents are not perfect but no adult cynicism can take away the memories of a loving childhood.

The Greeks called this Antanagoge

Far be it from me to say your feet stink!
The Greeks called this Apophasis.

Clever, sometimes aggressive, writers can state or give special emphasis to something by seeming to pointedly ignore it, pass over it, or deny it. A writer or speaker uses this device to avoid (or appear to avoid) offending holders of opposing ideas, while mentioning and calling attention to sensitive or inflammatory facts or statements. This device can be used effectively by speakers who are good enough actors to appear to be detached from the negative statements that are mentioned in passing in an off-hand way.

> *I will not mention the large budget problem that is ruining us, or how your department's unsuccessful programs have nearly pushed us into bankruptcy, because I am not looking to humiliate you.*

> *Li's proud adherence to his Chinese culture that stresses filial piety, must be judged in the light of the minimal care he provides for his father.*

> *It is not necessary to mention Peter's many scandals, both at home and abroad, nor the failed investments he involved his family in, nor his numerous litigations, since I want to concentrate not on the man but on the*

22

characteristics of the product that he is
currently sponsoring.

There is a fine line between the legitimate and the illegitimate use of this device. If it is employed to bring in irrelevant statements while it supplies a screen to hide behind, it is an abusive use. The first of the following examples clearly has the purpose of smearing the opponent. The second appears to be a serious consideration of the causes of a problem.

> *I will not repeat that Crump is a poor manager who is responsible for delays in production.*

> *I do not mean to suggest that Mr. Crump is the cause of the inefficiency and work blockage in this factory. I am looking for the reason for the correlation between the paperwork that goes through his office and the delays on the shop floor.*

The dishonest use of this device is common in political campaigns. Accusations are hinted at, and implied, and then followed by protestations of innocence.

Often the real purpose of saying, "I do not mean to suggest [or imply]" something is precisely to say it. We all know that if you throw enough mud, some of it sticks.

However, some honest writers and speakers use this expression or others like it to keep a discussion clear, and to emphasize what their real intentions are and

23

are not.

This literary/rhetorical tool is handy for reminding people of your views in a polite non-pushy way:

> *Of course, I do not need to mention that our sales staff should always be very well groomed.*

> *Our enthusiasm about natural gas as a clean fuel has nothing to do with our firm opposition to obtaining it by hydraulic fracturing with its attendant damage to the environment.*

Some useful phrases for this tool are:

nothing need be said about, I pass over, it need not be said (or mentioned), I will not mention (or dwell on or bring up), we will overlook, I do not mean to suggest (or imply), you need not be reminded, it is unnecessary to bring up, we can forget about, no one would suggest.

Remember, the Greeks called this Apophasis.

Well, maybe...
The Greeks called this Aporia.

෧෨

Sometimes writers and speakers want to express their current view of an issue without a final commitment to their position. They express doubt about an idea or conclusion. This device is a useful way to present alternatives without making a commitment to either or any:

> *I am not sure whether to side with those who say increased immigration will hurt the native born, or with those who say that more workers will increase demand and employment.*

> *To be, or not to be: that is the question.*
> *Whether 'tis nobler in the mind to suffer*
> *The slings and arrows of outrageous fortune,*
> **Hamlet, William Shakespeare**

> *I wonder about the value of dress codes, because I value the students' growth in decision making, as well as the need for decorum and respectability in our students' dress.*

This device is useful as a means to three ends:

1. It can help you to dismiss assertions that are irrelevant to the discussion without either conceding or denying the assertion.

2. It can put off a piece of discussion you do not have the time or desire to pursue,

3. It can begin treatment of an issue, and lead to a conclusion which resolves the doubt.

You can use aporia to cast doubt in a modest way, as a kind of understatement:

> *I am not so sure I can accept Pete's reasons for wanting another new car.*

> *I have not yet been fully convinced that driving is better than public transportation..*

> *I am not sure about the other reasons offered in favor of the new courthouse, but I am willing to be convinced.*

> *Yes, I know you both insist on saying that the valve can be opened. I do not know what to say about that. I only know that I could not open it.*

A skillful writer can use this device to express an ironic doubt about several closely debatable matters:

> *Whether he was better at convincing the simple to invest in his projects, impressing young women, or in producing superficial best sellers, I can't decide.*

> *Who enjoyed the summer afternoon most? John and Grace holding hands and talking sweet talk under the oak tree, or Grace's mother watching them through her window? I don't know.*

> *"Am I no better than a eunuch or is the proper man — the man with the right to existence — a raging stallion forever neighing after his neighbor's womankind? Or are we meant to act on impulse alone? It is all a darkness."*
> (Ford Maddox, The Good Soldier, 1915)

And you can display ignorance about something while really showing your belief and attitude about it or something else:

> *I am not sure why some people think that a city dweller's right to have an assault rifle is the hallmark of democracy.*

> *I have often wondered why my kids don't realize that those same sneakers are available*

27

for half the price under a different label.

I do not know whether this measure will work all the miracles promised by its adherents, but it does seem to merit more thought.

Remember the Greeks called this Aporia.

Purple People Eater
The Romans called this Distinctio.

A popular song of the 50s was "The Purple People Eaters". The public wondered was it about purple hued cannibals, or were they cannibals of any complexion that only ate purple people?

The participants in a conversation about the meaning of the song have to clarify (distinguish) between the two possible meanings of the term *Purple People Eater*. They need to use the literary device distinctio.

When there is a disagreement about the meaning of a word, it is necessary to make clear the differences between the possible meanings of the term. If you call a tomato a vegetable, I will use the literary device of *distinctio* to clarify that it is a fruit. Similarly, I must clarify that a peanut is not a nut but that it is a legume.

Distinctio is a literary and rhetorical strategy in which the writer or speaker gives more detail about the meaning of a word, to clear up any possible misunderstanding.

True champagne, by which I mean the sparkling wine from the Champagne region of France has yet to be successfully copied anywhere in the world.

We don't have much time, by that I mean fifty

years.

Is this model airplane easy to build? Can my 10 year old son do it or is it so difficult that he needs a degree in engineering?

It is sometimes necessary to insist on a particular meaning of a word or expression from among the possible various meanings, in order to remove or prevent ambiguity.

When engineers say that to make a car that gets 70 miles a gallon is impossible, they clarify that "impossible" means that it cannot be achieved without changing drastically our automobile design.

You're so ugly, you make onions cry.

The hydraulic cement has to be applied quickly. In conditions of normal humidity. "Quickly" means in less than four minutes.

Do not confuse motion *and* progress. *A rocking chair keeps moving but does not make any* progress.

The politician says that the reform is a simple one. If by simple he means not complicated, he is correct. If he means easy to implement, he is sadly mistaken.

Many of our words, like those that express a judgment (*better, failure, high quality, efficient, unacceptable*) and those referring to abstract concepts which are often debated (*democracy, justice, equality, oppression*) have different meanings for different people, and sometimes for the same person at different times.

For example, the governments of both The People's Republic of China and the United States call themselves "democracies," while it could be argued that neither really is a democracy.

The philosopher S. I. Hayakawa says "no word ever has exactly the same meaning twice". These words themselves may be an exaggeration in need of distinguishing the meaning of the word "never". However, we should remember that our words are flexible. When there might be some doubt about your meaning, it is good to clarify your statement or terms.

Remember the Romans called it Distinctio.

What if horses had feathers?

The Greeks called this Erotesis

Erotesis, or the *Rhetorical Question* a device that we use to awaken interest, express emotion and to infuse energy into our argument by asking questions.

The idea of this device is to call attention to the subject, and is a way to produce a powerful impression about the truth of a subject, as it implicitly rules out the possibility of contradiction.

The rhetorical question only differs from Q&A (**Hypophora**) on page 44 in that it is not answered by the writer. This is because its answer is obvious and is used not to get an answer but to cause an effect, stress, or provocation, or to wrap up an idea from the facts at hand.

The writer who uses the rhetorical question clearly signals that he has no doubt of the answer.

> *Is there any difference between the two U.S. political parties when both rely on campaign contributions?*

> *If we lose the ability to tell right from wrong, can our children acquire this ability?*

> *Is altruism only a word? Or is it present in our society today?*

Often the rhetorical question and its implied answer will lead to further discussion:

Is more and more buying of more and more stuff our unavoidable end? Is the shopping mall the highest accomplishment we can expect from our era? Maybe we should examine the alternatives presented by the people of other countries.

Sure, money is scarce, but shouldn't good projects be tried, even though they are not certain to succeed? [Note: The writer clearly wants the answer "yes", although someone might say "no" if asked directly. The rhetorical question is the cue for further discussion.

Several rhetorical questions together can form a nicely developed and directed paragraph by changing a series of logical statements into queries:

You are hesitant to approve changes, yet can there be any progress without change? Can we get the delicious fruit without losing the flower? Can we make a fire without destroying the wood? Can't you see that change in society is of the same nature and just as necessary as that of the natural world.

Sometimes the desired answer to the rhetorical question is made obvious by the discussion immediately preceding it:

You feel no resentment at having to put up eternally with the troubles and misdeeds of your children; you continue to show every possible care and concern for them. Should we then lose patience with the emotionally immature adults who also make our life difficult?

"Another thing that disturbs me about the American church is that you have a white church and a Negro church. How can segregation exist in the true Body of Christ?"

Martin Luther King, Jr. 1956

The use of this device allows you to lead your reader to think, wonder, and draw conclusions along with you; but if your questions become ridiculous, your writing will be ineffective and will not be appreciated.

Therefore, when you are thinking about using rhetorical questions, be careful with the use of the device.

We might ask, "Aren't we citizens; don't we have the right to protest?" An example of a poor use would be, "But don't we have the right to burn down the campus and sack the bookstore?"

Remember, the Greeks called this Erotesis.

Take My Wife...
The Romans called this Exemplum.

Exemplum: This device cites an example, using a story, either true or fictitious, that illustrates a point being made.

Exemplum is a widely used rhetorical devices. At first, it was employed by teachers and preachers in their writings and to guide audiences. Speakers and writers use historical figures as good and bad examples in order to encourage listeners to do good and avoid evil. It is used in everyday life as a basic method of argument.

Aristotle divided exemplum into two types:

Real Exemplum – from actual history. An article dealing with the financial crisis of 2008 might talk of the effects of the repeal of the Glass Steagall act to offer the following example of financial irresponsibility:

> *In the 1980's and 90's, the US government let the banks mix their speculative assets with the funds of their depositors. This led to nationwide financial ruin.*

Fictional Exemplum – from invented facts in parables, fables, brief comparisons etc. Children's stories abound in examples, such as George Washington and the cherry tree, Pinocchio's nose, etc.

This is a very straightforward and uncomplicated figure of speech. We use it all the time in teaching, presenting or defending our ideas. For this reason, this chapter will be very short as there is no need for examples of the figure of speech "example".

Examples can be introduced by the phrase, *For example,* but there are other ways of getting to the point of the example. For quick introductions you can begin a sentence or a phrase with: "such as," or "for instance."

Examples placed into separate sentences can be introduced by: "A case in point," "An instance," "A typical situation," "A common example," "To illustrate, let's consider the situation," and so forth.

Remember, the Romans called this Exemplum

He was ten feet tall!
The Greeks called this Hyperbole.

Hyperbole: We use this term in English in the same way the Greeks did, to indicate a deliberate exaggeration used for emphasis or effect. The skillful writer has to make it clear that it is an exaggeration, and should carefully restrict its use. Do not exaggerate everything, but treat hyperbole like a whistle to be blown only once a year. Then it will be quite effective as a way to get attention, a good way to lead into your essay or some part of it.

You can make a single point very emphatically:

> *There are a thousand reasons why you should vote for my candidate.*

Or you can exaggerate one thing to show that it is very different from something similar:

> *He said that his snake oil cures every ailment known to mankind.*

> *It was so cold I saw polar bears with earmuffs.*

> *She is as thin as a toothpick.*

You could have knocked me over with a feather when I saw what she did.

If I lose my keys, my mom is going to kill me.

Everybody knows that.

My mom works her fingers to the bone.

This restaurant's coffee is used motor oil next to the coffee my wife makes. (This sentence is also an analogy. See page 20

Hyperbole is the most overused and overdone literary and rhetorical device in the whole world. (OK, maybe that's a hyperbole!). Some writers like excess and exaggeration. Nevertheless, hyperbole still has a correct and useful place in speeches and in your writing.

Remember the Greeks called this Hyperbole.

Q and A
The Greeks called this Hypophora.

You can raise one or more questions and then go on to answer them even at some length. It's common to ask the question at the beginning of a paragraph and then answer the question in the rest of the paragraph:

A common use of this device is in paragraph introductions. You can begin the paragraph with a question, and then use the remaining space to answer that question. For example: *Why should we recycle? I'll give you five good reasons.*

This device is used all over the world on picket lines and in protest manifestations. The young people may not know they are using an ancient communication strategy, *hypophora*, when they chant, *"What do we want? BETTER TEACHERS! When do we want them? NOW!*

It also is used in political debates. *"What is the mayor doing about poverty in our city? He has raised taxes on the people driving pickup trucks and lowered taxes on the people riding in limousines."*

This is an attractive writing and speaking device, because asking an appropriate question appears quite natural and helps to maintain curiosity and interest. You can use it to raise questions which you think the reader obviously has on his mind and would like to see formulated and answered:

> *Aren't we all worried about additives in our food? Some nutritionists say the problem is much worse than we think.*

This tool can also be used to raise questions or to introduce material of weight, which the reader might not have knowledge of, or interest in:

> *Is the United States an empire? Empire is as empire does. The U.S. has thousands of military bases all over the world.*

> *Is it consistently hotter in Africa and the Amazon than anywhere else on earth? To experience the answer to this question, visit Texas in the summer.*

A question followed by an answer can be used as a transitional or signaling device to change directions or to enter a new area of discussion:

> *What are the implications of string theory? They are many and not all are the exclusive business of theoretical physicists; let's look at some implications that hit all of us in our daily life.*

Richard Nordquist gives us the following inspiring examples in *http://grammar.about.com/*.

"There are those who are asking the devotees of civil rights, 'When will you be satisfied?' We can never be satisfied as long as the Negro is the victim of the unspeakable horrors of police brutality. We can never be satisfied as long as our bodies, heavy with the fatigue of travel, cannot gain lodging in the motels of the highways and the hotels of the cities. We cannot be satisfied as long as the Negro's basic mobility is from a smaller ghetto to a larger one. We can never be satisfied as long as our children are stripped of their self- hood and robbed of their dignity by a sign stating 'For Whites Only.' We cannot be satisfied as long as a Negro in Mississippi cannot vote and a Negro in New York believes he has nothing for which to vote. No, no, we are not satisfied, and we will not be satisfied..."
Martin Luther King, Jr., "I Have a Dream," August 1963

"What kind of peace do I mean and what kind of a peace do we seek? Not a Pax Americana enforced on the world by American weapons of war. Not the peace of the grave or the security of the slave. I am talking about genuine peace, the kind of peace that makes life on earth worth living..."
John F. Kennedy, address at American University, 1963

Sometimes the same effect can be achieved by asking a follow-up question which serves as a restatement of the first question. These questions can keep a discussion lively and interesting.

42

The following words at a global meeting resounded all over the world in 2012. The important content and fervent emotion of the speech were supported by the use of hypophora. Naderev Sano, the lead negotiator of the Philippines delegation speaking at global climate summit in Doha, Qatar, December 12, 2012, ended his speech with:

> ""*I ask of all of us here, if not us, then* **who?** *If not now, then when? If not here, then where?*" **Naderev Sano**

Similarly, another political address which uses follow-up questions and a restatement of the writer's underlying views demonstrates the effectiveness of hypophora.

> *How do we know that the proposed immigration strategy is the best, particularly in view of the complaints that citizen groups have made against it? Isn't there some chance that greater penalties would amount to greater deterrents? Why not get the most border protection simultaneously with the most punishment to offenders? It happens that that's been tried, and it didn't work very well.*

Remember, the Greeks called this Hypophora.

Corn is not scarce in Iowa

The Greeks called this Litotes

You can use a special form of understatement by denying the opposite or contrary of the main idea in your argument. If not used carefully it can confuse a poor reader. But an advanced reader will appreciate the form and will receive a more impactful delivery of your idea. Compare the following:

> *Rain is common in April in New York City. Rain is not rare in April in New York City.*

Sometimes, by using this form, you can show restraint and modesty in expressing your views.

> *I believe that buying this car would not be a bad idea.*
>
> *To my surprise, the meal I cooked was not difficult to eat.*

Usually though, this construction makes the writer's case more forcefully, and shows strong feelings communicated in a calm way.

> *Marrying that man will not be the end of your troubles.*

To make unwanted sexual advances is no small matter.

But do not overdo the use of the prefixes "un" and "dis" A good writer will search for the word that is opposite to his thought. Although to write "not unwilling" might be a good way to describe the one person in a group who is in favor of an idea that is being discussed, in other cases it might be better to just write "willing". But many times, it is better to use a thesaurus to find the right word instead of writing "~~unnegative~~" or "~~disprepared~~" or other clumsy expressions.

When Pliny was entrusted with the government of Bithynia and Pontus, provinces by no means the richest or most considerable of the empire, he found the cities within his jurisdiction striving with each other in every useful and ornamental work...
Gibbon, The Decline and Fall of the Roman Empire

But if the emperors were the first, they were not the only architects of their dominions as their example was universally imitated by their principal subjects, who were not afraid of declaring to the world that they had spirit to conceive, and wealth to accomplish, the noblest undertakings.
Gibbon, The Decline and Fall of the Roman Empire

Remember, the Greeks called this Litotes

I Changed My Mind!
The Greeks called this Metanoia.

This is the exact term used in the Greek New Testament that is translated as *repentance*.

Often a writer qualifies a statement by retracting it (or part of it) and expressing it in a different way, in a better, milder, or stronger way. The recall is usually signified by a strong negative:

> *Diego was the best forward on the team, no, the best in the league.*

> *The most important thing to look for in tongue and groove flooring is hardness; no, not so much hardness as close tight grain..*

The *pasteles* of Doña Zoila are the best in New York. No, Are you kidding? The best in Spanish Harlem, Puerto Rico, and all the Caribbean!

Metanoia, much as other devices, can be used to bring the reader into broadening her belief or understanding:

> *These new sewers will improve the drainage of our streets, or rather the general public health of the whole district.*

Metanoia can be a way of persuading your reader of your point of view.

First you make a mildly controversial statement, then you change it to make it stronger.

This is a slower way of arguing rather than making the stronger claim on its own. Or in reverse the stronger claim may be stated first but then lowered to something less striking that is easier to accept.

"Metanoia can create an impression of scrupulousness, as the speaker starts to say one thing but then feels obliged to take the initiative in correcting it. (It also can suggest over scrupulousness, as when the speaker fusses too much.)" **(Ward Farnsworth, *Farnworth's Classical English Rhetoric*. David Godine, 2011) quoted by Norquist in *grammar.about.com***

Or it can be used to moderate and nuance an extreme expression (while, of course, retaining the impact of the extreme expression for good effect):

> *While the potholes riddle our streets and ruin our cars, the city bureaucrats just look on twiddling their thumbs, more interested in their careers and salaries than in the well-being of the city they have sworn to serve. This the impression we get from their*

47

inaction.

Besides *"no"*, other words and phrases such as the following are useful for this device: *rather, at least, let us say, I should say, I mean, to be more exact, or better, or rather, or maybe.*

Remember the Greeks called this Metanoia.

A Stitch in Time...
The Romans called this Sententia.

This device involves the quoting a maxim or wise saying to apply a general truth to the situation; concluding or summing up your thoughts by offering a single, pithy statement of general wisdom. Sententia can be used not only to or sum up a discussion but also can be used to lead into a further treatment of an issue.

A careful use of sententia can give authority to your writing; and excessive use can make your arguments sound "preachy" or weak and in need of support. This was commented on 2000 years ago.

"It is best to insert sententiae discreetly, that we may be viewed as judicial advocates, not moral instructors." **(Rhetorica ad Herennium, c. 90 BC)**

Sententia is often introduced with phrases such: "As so- and-so (once) said", "According to so-and-so" and "In the (famous) words of so-and-so ...".

> *The realist says that to understand politics, "Follow the Money."*

> *But, of course, to understand all is to forgive all.*

As the saying goes, art is long and life is short.

For as Pascal reminds us, "It is not good to have all your wants satisfied."

My grandmother always said, "Seeing is believing".

Hercule Poirot reminds us to, "cherchez la femme."

Sententia usually comes at the end of the argument to help summarize and reinforce it in a powerful way.

I am not a perfect servant. I am a public servant doing my best against the odds. As I develop and serve, be patient: God is not finished with me yet. **Jesse Jackson,** *1984* **Democratic National Convention**

"So, I'm happy tonight. I'm not worried about anything. I'm not fearing any man. 'Mine eyes have seen the glory of the coming of the Lord.'"
Martin Luther King, Jr., *I've Been to the Mountaintop*

"The lesson we have to learn is that our dislike for certain persons does not give us any right to injure our fellow creatures. The social rule must be: Live and let live."
George Bernard Shaw

Sometimes proverbs are a convenient way to deliver a sententia. They have the advantage of being familiar and are usually accepted without discussion.

The squeaky wheel gets the grease.

People who live in glass houses shouldn't throw stones.

Better late than never.

Birds of a feather flock together.

A picture is worth a thousand words.

There's no place like home.

The early bird gets the worm.

A penny saved is a penny earned.

You can get more "bang for the buck" out of a few words by using sententia in your writing. You can touch common chords in your readers' minds, and lead them to concentrate on your train of thought.

Remember the Romans called this Sententia.

A String of Pearls.

The Greeks called this Scesis Onomaton.

A good writer can call attention to an idea by repeating the core idea expressing it in a series of generally synonymous phrases or statements. This is an obvious manipulation of words, and therefore it should be used carefully so as to not call attention to itself rather than to the ideas that are emphasized. If done right, this deliberate and obvious restatement can be quite effective:

> *He lied, he prevaricated, he bent the truth, when in doubt he gave in to mendacity.*

> *We succeeded, we were victorious, we accomplished the feat!*

> *Veni, vidi, vinci*

> *I came, I saw, I conquered* Julius Caesar

> *Ah sinful nation, a people laden with iniquity, a seed of evildoers, children that deal corruptly.* Isaiah 1:4

> *But there is one thing these blue-sky planners forget: their plan is extremely costly, tremendously expensive, and requires*

collecting more tax revenue.

The fairy princess lay there, motionless in a peaceful slumber, in complete quietude, in the arms of sleep.

Some students of writing say that this tool is showy and that it calls attention to itself, and can appear repetitive, so it is not used as frequently in formal writing as some other devices. I disagree. I think that if well done, it is strikingly emphatic.

Remember, the Greeks called this Scesis Onomaton.

Aw Shucks! I only know a little...

Understatement

You can make a statement in your writing by deliberately presenting an idea as less meaningful than it really is, either with irony or by restraint.

When your audience probably knows the truth about a subject that is difficult to describe well in a short space, you can understate the fact. This gives your reader the satisfaction of using their own knowledge and judgment.

For example, it would be difficult to describe in a few words the horrors and destruction of the terrible Fukushima earthquake and tsunami. Using the device of understatement, you might write:

> *The events in Fukushima clearly affected the Japanese economy in 2011 and in subsequent years.*

The effect is not the same as a full description of the destruction. It is true that understatements like this sometimes might appear to lack feeling for the tragedy.
However, when used correctly, it avoids the opposite error of giving superfluous detail about a subject that is well known. Look at these examples from English literature.

Henry and Catherine were married, the bells rang, and everybody smiled ...To begin perfect happiness at the respective ages of twenty-six and eighteen is to do pretty well... Jane Austen

Last week I saw a woman flayed, and you will hardly believe how much it altered her person for the worse. Jonathan Swift

In the two examples of above, the writers use understatement to express irony. Austen conveys a controlled joy and happiness, and Swift expresses outrage and anger.

In these examples of understatement, the reader brings his own knowledge of the facts, and possibly imagines a stronger and more personal description than the writer might have.

In a more personal way, you might use understatement as a way to be modest in your writing. Whenever you have to write about your own accomplishments or describe your own position, to understate the facts will help you to avoid the charge of egoism or self praise. It is better to have your readers discover more than they expect rather than find less than they expect.

You will be more admired as a writer if the readers find about your talents on their own. An experienced politician might say,

Yes, I know a little about public opinion, rather than,

Yes, because of my experience of 20 years in politics I am an expert in the history and study of public opinion...

It is useful to use understatement when dealing with a hostile audience or when disagreeing with an accepted opinion or belief. You can say the same in a less offensive way. Compare:

The evidence for the fact of climate change seems to contradict the Republican position.

The evidence for climate change proves conclusively that the Republican position is utterly false and ridiculous.

If you as a writer want to persuade a reader, once you insult or mock her, you will never persuade her of anything, no matter how "obviously wrong" she is or how clearly right you are. You must never underestimate the power of pride and "face" in your reader.

By using understatement in the right place in your writing, you show respect for your readers' understanding.

Although you object to their belief, you show respect for their position and how they came to believe it.

You carefully try to put the reader right, or offer a more accurate view. Look at the following contrasting approaches to disagreeing.

The person who says that our meat inspection is safe is either ignorant or corrupted by the meat packing industry.

Some people say that the meat we eat is inspected but I'm not so sure. Maybe they have not seen the recent information about the deregulation of the meat packing process and the cutting of thousands of inspectors.

Remember, we call this "Understatement"

Chapter Two:

Organization and Arrangement

The following is a good example of a literary device that uses words to arrange the ideas in one's writing, not only for easier understanding but also for a pleasant effect. We will see others of different types in the following chapter

With malice toward none; With charity for all; With firmness in the right,...
Abraham Lincoln, Second Inaugural Address

.

Loose Cannons
The Greeks called this Asyndeton No connectors

Your writing can appear more lively and vigorous if occasionally you leave out the word "and" or other connecting words between words, phrases, or clauses. Omitting the connectors in a list of items can also give the impression of an amount too big to be counted.

Sometimes a list with no connector communicates a strong finish to the list and garners much more attention than if a final conjunction were used.

> *The researchers worked all night reading, comparing, thinking, understanding.*

Sometimes, the omission of a conjunction between short phrases gives the impression of the phrases having the same meaning or a close relation. In the following sentences, the use of the word "and" gives the idea that you are writing about two separate qualities of the person, while the omission of "and" presents the idea of the integration of the virtues of the person.

> *He was a champion, a hero.*

> *He was a champion and a hero.*

Leaving out the link can show more naturalness and ease of expression.

"The perfect, shining, green leaf" appears more natural and spontaneous than "The perfect, shining and green leaf".

Generally, you can write in a way that offers the feeling of speed and preciseness to lists and phrases and clauses. It usually is a pleasant effect, even if we don't know why, but this is your privilege as a writer: that of creating the impression that you want.

Remember, the Greeks called this Asyndeton

Black and White
The Greeks called this Antithesis

Often a good writer establishes a clear, contrast two ideas by joining them together or putting one next to the other, often in parallel structure. It is known to be a sign of intelligence to be able to systematize and categorize things, so you can show your intelligence and appeal to the intelligence of your reader, by using contrast which creates a definite and systematic relationship between ideas:

> *When the going is tough, the tough get going. To err is human; to forgive, divine.*
> **An Essay on Criticism, Alexander Pope (1688-1744)**

> *That's one small step for a man, one giant leap for mankind.* **Neil Armstrong**

> *The bigger the peppermill, the worse the restaurant.*

> *It was the best of times; it was the worst of times.*
> **Tale of Two Cities, Dickens**

You can get across an idea of complexity in a person or idea by emphasizing opposite or nearly opposite characteristics of that person or idea:

We tend to believe that milk builds strong bones, but many doctors say the opposite is true.

Television brings the world to our living room but destroys community connections.

Sometimes it is necessary to make precise contrasts, fine distinctions, or careful distinctions. This is the job of the writer who must be thinking of the possible careless reader of his work:

There is a difference between the economical and the cheap.

It may be legal for corporations to avoid paying taxes but it is not patriotic

I will fight against your political views but I will fight for you to have the right to express them.

See also the related rhetorical device **distinctio.**

Short phrases can also be used to show contrast:

Whoever wants to grow tomatoes should prepare the soil, choose good seedlings, plant them carefully, fertilize them lightly, tie them carefully to stakes, water them regularly, and remember that success depends on good practices and that not following these practices will never bring bounteous harvests.

Listen, young men, to an old man to whom old men were glad to listen when he was young.
Augustus

Songwriters and other artists are skillful at using contrast in their work:

Hot N' Cold, by Katy Perry

'cause you're hot, then you're cold
You're yes then you're no
You're in then you're out
You're up then you're down
You're wrong when it's right
It's black and it's white
We fight, we break up
We kiss, we make up

"I would rather be ashes than dust! I would rather that my spark should burn out in a brilliant blaze than it should be stifled by dry rot. I would rather be a superb meteor, every atom of me in magnificent glow, than a sleepy and permanent planet. The proper function of man is to live, not to exist. I shall not waste my days in trying to prolong them. I shall use my time."
Jack London

Remember, the Greeks called this Antithesis

Criss Cross
The Greeks called this Antimetabole

A clever arrangement of words is pleasant to read, and can add to the impact of your writing. However, it cannot be a puzzle; it must be clear.

You can learn to use repeating words in successive clauses, but in transposed order. In other words you balance the second half of an expression against the first but with the words in reverse grammatical order

The letters A,B, stand for words or expressions. These words or expressions can be represented as A-B, B-A. So, a simple example: fish and chips & chips and fish

In a real expression, this device intensifies the final expression, presents alternatives, or shows contrast:

> *Eat to live, not live to eat.* Socrates

> *I know what I like, and I like what I know.*

> *Ask not what your country* can do for *you*; ask what *you* can *do for your country*."
> John F. Kennedy, Inauguration, Jan. 20, 1961.

> *When the going gets tough, the tough get going.*

"You stood up for America, now America must stand up for you."
Barack Obama - December 14, 2011.

"We didn't land on Plymouth Rock. Plymouth Rock landed on us."
Malcolm X

I can hit better than anybody who can run faster, and I can run faster than anybody who can hit better. **José Pierre Murphy Cohen**

For antimetaboles to be effective, they have to be grammatically correct and also should be logical. Don't think you can produce them without much thought.. To be a good antimetabole the crisscross must be logical.

Remember the Greeks called this Antimetabole

Bookends

The Greeks called this Epanalepsis.

You can repeat the beginning word of a clause or sentence at the end of the same clause or sentence. Since the beginning and the end are the two positions of strongest significance in a sentence, if you place the same word in both places of the expression, it gets special attention.

Words at the beginning are remembered because of the "first punch" effect, while words at the end are remembered more often because of the "last punch" effect. Putting the same words at the start and at the end gets a "one-two punch" effect

> *Ice cream: you scream, we all scream for Ice Cream!*
>
> *Religion helps many people while many others are harmed by religion.*
>
> *To err is human, but a human approaches the divine by trying not to err.*
>
> *The king is dead; long live the king!*
> **Old English Expression**

The purpose of this device to send two messages

66

between the "bookends", the beginning and end of the expression:

- to mention a well-accepted fact and
- to place the fact in context.

Many people loudly announce their principles but the slightest inconvenience leads them to abandon these same principles.

Agreement in a crisis is hard to attain, although often the only way out of the crisis is by reaching agreement. .

In the world you have tribulation, but take courage; I have overcome the world. John 16:33

Remember, the Greeks called this Epanalepsis.

To dig I am not able...
The Greeks called this Hyperbaton.

Hyperbaton is a strategy which alters the normal position of words, phrases and clauses and creates differently arranged sentences with the same meaning but with different effect and emphasis. It effects a more complex and intriguing sentence structure that can add depth and interest to the expression of the thought.

There are several ways to change normal word order. One way is for the adjective to follow the noun. If you want to stress the adjective, this inverted order is very useful.

Special punctuation is not necessary but a comma before a following adjective can help the sense.

> *From his window he saw the abandoned girl, content with her new doll.*

> *It was a long lecture but interesting.*

> *Her ideal was a car big and blue.*

> *The shingles needed big nails, heavy-duty style.*

> *Snow, extremely heavy broke the cabin's roof.*

You can also stress priority by putting a verb at the end of the sentence, as in the following examples:

> *We will not, from this conviction, for any reason, be dissuaded.*

> *Pete, after running the marathon, crossed the line and collapsed.*

> *Some rise by sin, and some by virtue fall....*
> **Measure for Measure by William Shakespeare**

Another form of hyperbaton involves the separation of words normally belonging together:

> *In this assembly there sit twenty (and it has been confirmed) traitorous members.*

> *Alone sat the child in the corner of the classroom.*

Be careful with this device. If "funny, it sounds" you better rewrite it. But don't give up on this twist in your writing just because at first you find it challenging. There can be opportunities worthy of this device.

Remember the Greeks called this Hyperbaton.

Railroad Tracks
Parallelism

This feature of good writing is more than just a stylistic touch; it is considered by many to be a requirement of good writing style. It is the use of the same or similar grammatical structures in different parts of phrase. Several parts of a phrase, sentence or several sentences are expressed similarly to show that the ideas in the parts or sentences contribute equally to the thought. Parallelism can also add balance and rhythm and, most importantly, clarity to the sentence.

One effect of parallelism in your writing is to help your readers follow your ideas. It also is pleasing to the mind and the ear to read and hear a well-built sentence that shows that the writer has worked at having their ideas lined up and related correctly to each other.

An example of parallelism is the ancient and widespread European proverb about the *Gardener's Dog* who "doesn't eat nor lets others eat."

Good writing matches up words and phrases according to their grammar and logic. For example, it is poor writing to say, "~~I like eating cake and to drink coffee.~~" This mixes a participle (the word with "ing") and an infinitive (beginning with "to").

It would be better to write either of the following sentences:

> *I like eating cake and drinking coffee. I like to eat cake and to drink coffee.*

Any part of a sentence can be paralleled.

Subjects:

> *Dangerous animals and poisonous plants are part of the charm of* my backyard.

Parallel verbs and adverbs:

> *He has always started his diets with enthusiasm but has seldom finished one with results.*

Parallel verbs and direct objects:

> *He wanted to drink rum and to eat coconuts.*

Just the objects:

> *The industrious housewife washed the windows, the rug, and the tub, all in three hours.*

Parallel phrases:

> *The pilot showed off his skill, climbing vertically and diving rapidly.*

> *To eat right and to exercise regularly are the pillars of health.*

> *She liked walking in the rain and kicking the puddles.*

> *He didn't know if he should vote for his brother or for the better candidate .*

Your writing will be clearer if you make long subordinate clauses parallel. This helps the reader keep track of our argument.

> *After you sauté the onions which you just bought, but before you add the garlic that your brother-in- law brought with him, chop up the meat.*

In summary, you can make parallel many combination of parts of speech or sentence, depending on your intended content and intent sought.

Here are some classical examples of parallelism:

> *(I hope) I can be numbered among the writers who have given ardor to virtue, and confidence to truth.*
> **Samuel Johnson**

> *They had great skill in optics, and had instructed him to see faults in others, and beauties in himself, that could be discovered by nobody else.* **Alexander Pope**

> *The end of a theoretical science is truth, but the end of a practical science is performance.*
> **Aristotle**

Parallelism is so important to your writing that you should do the following exercise.

Improve the parallelism of these sentences. The corrections follow.

1. The Director told the staff to collect the material and get to work and that the original provisions would apply.

2. Finding the answers to his questions was not difficult, but to convince him of the rightness of them was a superhuman task.

3. All of these people were given training in handling investigative reports and how to interpret the conclusions.

4. Actually it was not only a matter of excessive expenditures of money and poor planning, because no one had ever attempted to plan the program within available resources.

5. The instructor will develop how you pronounce words, your voice modulation, and he will notice your hand gestures.

6. He is a hardworking, conscientious employee who cooperates well.

7: The director is interested neither in corresponding with them nor does he want to view their display.

8. She served as the secretary for two years, as the treasurer for three years, and for two years she was the president.

9. We want you to design a workbook, select a text and a starting date should be determined.

10. I went not only to see him but also because I wanted to look for a job.

11. The secretary is good at filing, spelling, writing, and she likes to type.

12. He gave instructions first to check the work thoroughly and then for revising it.

13. This new product offers these advantages—easy operation, durability, and is economical.

Parallelism Exercise: Corrections

1. The Director told the staff to collect the material, to work, and to apply the original provisions.

2. Finding the answers to his questions was not difficult, but to convince him of their rightness was a superhuman task.

3. All of these people were given training in handling investigative reports and in interpreting the conclusions.

4. Actually it was not only a matter of excessive expenditures of money, but also of poor planning, because no one had ever attempted to plan the program within available resources.

5. The instructor will develop your pronunciation, your voice modulation, and your hand gestures.

6. He is a hardworking, conscientious, cooperative employee.

7: The director is neither interested in corresponding with them nor viewing their display.

8. She served as the secretary for two years, as the treasurer for three years, and as president for two years.

9. We want you to design a workbook, select a text, and determine a starting date.

10. I went not only to see him but also to look for a job.

11. The secretary is good at filing, spelling, writing, and typing.

12. He gave instructions to first check the work thoroughly and then to revise it.

13. This new product offers these advantages—easy operation, durability, and economy.

The Cart Before The Horse

The Greeks called this Chiasmus

You know that you can add interest to your writing by using Parallelism, as seen in the previous device. You can also use Reverse Parallelism. For example, look at this parallel sentence: *"What is created with difficulty is not destroyed easily,"*

The arrangement is a simple parallel construction. The phrase *"created with difficulty"* is paralleled by another phrase *"not destroyed easily"*.

The two phrases *"created with difficulty"* and *"not destroyed easily"* complement (complete) the noun phrase *"What is created"*.

What is "reverse parallelism"? The writing/speaking device that we are looking at now, Chiasmus, is a parallel construction that relates the first part of a grammatical construction with the second part **in reverse order**.

Some writers, using Chiasmus, might choose not to use strict parallelism. They might prefer to write *"created with difficulty"* followed by *"not easily destroyed"*.

77

So instead of writing, "What is created with difficulty is not destroyed easily", you could write "What is created with difficulty is not easily destroyed."

Similarly, the parallel sentence, "The fields that are presently soaked were previously parched." could be written in reverse order, as, "The fields now soaked were parched before."

Here are other examples:

> *Never let a fool kiss you or a kiss fool you.*

> *Polished in courts and hardened in the field, renowned for conquest, and in council skilled.*
> **The English essayist, Joseph Addison**

> *For the Lord is a Great God ... in whose hand are the depths of the earth; the peaks of the mountains are his also.* **Psalm 95:4**

> *Many useful citizens are lawyers, but not all lawyers are useful citizens.*

Your writing can be made more interesting and engaging simply by moving subordinate clauses around. In the following sentence good people are praised for their many qualities:

If you come to them, they are not asleep; if you ask and inquire of them, they do not withdraw themselves; they do not chide if you make mistakes; they do not laugh at you if you are ignorant. **The medieval monk and librarian Richard de Bury**

Sometimes the effect is subtle and hard to define but pleasing. Do you feel the difference in these sentences?

> *During his youth he worked in a gas station and he fixed flats to pay for his books.*

> *During his youth he worked in a gas station and to pay for his books, he fixed flats.*

> *When anyone listens to them, they are full of ideas but when they have the chance to put these ideas in practice, they don't know what to do.*

> *When anyone listens to them, they are full of ideas but they don't know what to do when they have the chance to put these ideas in practice.*

Everyone has heard the criss-cross expression:
We must eat to live but the glutton lives to eat.

Chiasmus can help you change the direction and strength of the ingredients of a thought while avoiding the stiffness of a strict parallel arrangement, such as the one described on page 77

Remember, the Greeks called this Chiasmus.

Up, up and away...

The Greeks called this Climax,
and The Romans called it Gradatio.

Climax or Gradatio consists of arranging words, clauses, or sentences in the order of increasing importance, weight, or emphasis.

This progressive arrangement of parts of a sentence gradually (why the Romans called it Gradatio) builds to a major point (why the Greeks called it Climax).

> *We shall go on to the end. We shall fight in France, we shall fight on the seas and oceans, we shall fight with growing confidence and growing strength in the air, we shall defend our island, whatever the cost may be. We shall fight on the beaches, we shall fight on the landing grounds, we shall fight in the fields and in the streets, we shall fight in the hills; we shall never surrender...* **Churchill, June 4, 1940, House of Commons**

> *The spoken word recital, "My Aunt's Feet", was honored in The Bronx, they loved it in Union Square, it was used in hundreds of resamples in the Hip Hop community, the poet Bratty Stink felt it was his best work, and*

80

it appears that it will soon be considered as one of the planet's greatest artistic creations of the twentieth century.

We can learn a lot from this this progressive arrangement of parts of a sentence. It can help us in our other writing by reminding us that the impact of the gradual increase of intensity can also be used in longer pieces of writing.

Besides arranging sentences or groups of short ideas in progressive order, good writers can also arrange large sections of the arguments in their works climactically, that is leading up to the point to be made.

You can practice this also in your writing, always beginning with a point or proof that is important enough to awaken interest, and then continuing with elements of increasing weight. This device in your longer writing makes your argument stronger as it moves along, and every point has more impact than the previous one.

Remember The Greeks called this Climax and The Romans called it Gradatio

I came; I Saw; I conquered
The Greeks called this Parataxis

Parataxis describes the writing in which phrases or clauses are arranged independently, with no indication of level or subordination.

The original meaning of the Greek is clear: "placing side by side"

This device is still widely used in modern literature. Parataxis in writing refers to the use of simple declarative sentences or independent clauses, strung side by side. You can use it effectively in your writing. It is easy to grasp the idea and easy to use (and abuse — so use carefully!)

Since it is so useful, here is a little more explanation: By using parataxis you can get across the relation among ideas, emotions, or settings without specifically making the connection.

Each sentence reinforces the impression made by the previous one, creating a powerful overall effect. Instead of mixing longer and shorter sentences,

Parataxis places together a series of clauses that can stand alone. The separate clauses work together and explain each other as one idea.

Julius Caesar aptly summed the result of a battle with the paratactic declaration *"I came, I saw, I conquered."*

In spoken language, the flow from sentence to sentence is helped by intonation and timing (rhythm, pause). You can communicate this in your writing with parataxis.

However in poetry very different images or fragments, are placed together without a clear connection. Readers find pleasure in making their own connections.

In your writing you can communicate dependence without stating it clearly.

This sometimes has a powerful effect. You can write: "Hurricane Sandy, flooded us, knocked down our houses, we ate cold food, we walked around in blankets, we finally got to know our neighbors.

It is not necessary to say, "It was raining heavily so we stayed inside." The same message is understood when you write, "It was raining heavily, we stayed inside."

It is a useful device in describing a setting. "Verdant ferns, rippling water, sun dappled meadows, a haven for lovers"

Clear rhythm and repetition in paratactic language can communicate a focused, tense state of mind.

Repetition can also indicate a moment in time when everything seems to happen all at once.

Examples from literature.

"I came; I saw; I conquered." **Julius Caesar**

"...with no past, no language, no tribe, no source, no faded postcard" **Sula, Toni Morrison**

"I needed a drink, I needed a lot of life insurance, I needed a vacation, I needed a home in the country. What I had was a coat, a hat and a gun."
Farewell, My Lovely, Raymond Chandler

"I was late to meet someone but I stopped at Lexington Avenue and bought a peach and stood on the corner eating it and knew that I had come out of the West and reached the mirage."
Slouching Towards Bethlehem, Joan Didion

"Dogs, undistinguishable in mire. Horses, scarcely better.—splashed to their very blinkers. Foot passengers, jostling one another's umbrellas, in a general infection of ill-temper, and losing their foothold at street

corners. " **Charles Dickens, Bleak House, 1852-1853**

"In the bed of the river there were pebbles and boulders, dry and white in the sun, and the water was clear and swiftly moving and blue in the channels."
A Farewell to Arms, Ernest Hemingway

Remember the Greeks called this Parataxis

Parenthesis: *Those curvy things*
The Greeks called this Parenthesis, so do we.

The word *parenthesis* means "to place next to" in Greek. This note of "being extra" has survived from the Greeks to our time. The basic function of this figure of speech is to add something extra to a thought.

Sometimes we insert a word, phrase, or whole sentence in the middle of another sentence:

The impact on the reader of the author's jumping into (or out of) the middle of a sentence to clarify something is a powerful one. These parenthetical remarks can be set off by commas, dashes — for a greater effect — or by parentheses (to make your interruption more gentle).

> *But the new studies—which help us see the value of good statistics—show that better sales are possible with this design.*

> *And remember that life's A Great Balancing Act.*
> *And will you succeed?*
> *Yes! You will, indeed!*
> *(98 and ¾ percent guaranteed)*
> *KID, YOU'LL MOVE MOUNTAINS!*
> **(Dr. Seuss, *Oh, The Places You'll Go!* 1990)**

It is now necessary to warn you that your concern for the reader must be pure: you must sympathize with the reader's plight (most readers are in trouble about half the time) but never seek to know the reader's wants. Your whole duty as a writer is to please and satisfy yourself, and the true writer always plays to an audience of one.
(William Strunk, Jr. and E.B. White, *The Elements of Style.* **Allyn & Bacon, 1995)**

"Get your facts first, and then you can distort them as much as you please. (Facts are stubborn, but statistics are more pliable.)" **(Mark Twain)**

Every time I try jump rope, you guessed it, I fall on my behind.

Joe, a great hitter, was not a good fielder.

The wife (not her husband) is the boss of the house

As the earthy portion has its origin from earth, the watery from a different element, my breath from one source and my hot and fiery parts from another of their own elsewhere (for nothing comes from nothing, or can return to nothing), so too there must be an origin for the mind. **Marcus Aurelius**

The use of this device creates the effect of your thoughts being extemporaneous and relevant. Your reader sees that you are relating some fact when suddenly something very important comes to your mind, so you cannot resist a quick remark. To stop the sentence and the thought you are on to jump to another fact or comment gives this fact or comment special salience.

Remember the Greeks called this Parenthesis

Beads in a Chain:

Extra Connectors The Greeks called this Polysyndeton

This writing tool brings across a feeling of counting, of increase, and relation among the parts of the sentence or list.

> *He laughed and talked and smoked and drank. They read and reviewed and revised and wrote.*

> *To have the right principles, and to teach according to them, and to help all students towards them according to their abilities, this is what makes a great high school.*

> *We don't have money, nor family connections, nor influential friends, nor fancy degrees.*

You can write with extra connectors to cover something complex. Read how these poets do it:

> *The water, like a witch's oils, Burnt green, and blue, and white.*
> **S. T. Coleridge**

[He] pursues his way, and swims, or sinks, or wades, or creeps, or flies.
John Milton

The repeated connectors call attention to themselves and therefore add the effect of persistence or intensity or weight to the basic effect of repetition. When you use "and" repeatedly you stress the force of the argument at hand. The repeated use of "nor" or "or" *emphasizes alternatives. The repeated use of "but" or "yet" stresses reflection* or contrast. Consider the effectiveness of these:

Below are a few excellent examples given by Liz Bureman in the blog *The Write Practice*.

Example from Charles Dickens' *A Tale of Two Cities*:

> *... Jerry stood: aiming at the prisoner the beery breath of a whet he had taken as he came along, and discharging it to mingle with the waves of other beer,* and *gin,* and *tea,* and *coffee,* and *what not, that flowed at him, and already broke upon the great windows behind him in an impure mist and rain.*

A bit gross, but you get the idea.

The following example is from Mark Twain's *The Adventures of Huckleberry Finn:*

I got into my old rags and my sugar-hogshead again, and was free and satisfied. But Tom Sawyer he hunted me up and said he was going to start a band of robbers, and I might join if I would go back to the widow and be respectable. So I went back.

Twain was a big fan of polysyndeton and the first pages of Huckleberry Finn are littered with extra conjunctions.

Example from Jane Austen's *Pride and Prejudice*:

Mrs. Hurst and her sister allowed it to be so—but still they admired her and liked her, and pronounced her to be a sweet girl, and one whom they would not object to know more of.

Austen uses polysyndeton frequently to convey a sense of enthusiasm and breathlessness.

Example from Herman Melville's *Moby Dick*:

There was a low rumbling of heavy sea-boots among the benches, and a still slighter shuffling of women's shoes, and all was quiet again, and every eye on the preacher.

In this selection, Melville is constantly carried away by polysyndeton, which adds to the gravity of his prose.

Remember, the Greeks called this Polysyndeton

Verbal Hiccup
The Grammarians call this the Sentential Adverb.

This device (a handy trick) is a single word or short phrase, which interrupts the normal flow of a sentence and lends emphasis to the words next to it.

Compare these two sentences:

> *The house was not built before the summer.*
> *The house was not, in fact, built before the summer.*

In the second sentence, the words "not" and "built" are emphasized

Interruptions are most frequently placed near the beginning of a sentence, where important material has been placed:

> *As a matter of fact, the woman was not qualified.*

Or you can show that you do understand the significance of an argument even while rejecting it.

> *Obviously, we need petroleum for our energy, but we must control its use to protect our planet.*

Sometimes with short sentences, the interrupter can be placed last:

He won anyway.
It is hot in July, of course.

You may set off the interrupter adverb with commas.

He, clearly, is a man of honor.

An interrupter can emphasize an element of the sentence:

NOUN: *Fido, clearly a healthy puppy, now chases cars.*

VERB: *Fido, clearly a healthy puppy, now chases, but never catches, cars.*

ADJECTIVE: *Fido, clearly a healthy, very healthy, puppy, now chases cars.*

ADVERB: *Fido, clearly a healthy puppy, now, and for quite a while now, chases cars.*

You can use different punctuation to set off the interrupter:

We find a few people, however, always annoying. "Your last opera," he said, "is a masterpiece."

A good cake—as you know—needs butter in abundance.

They will (I trust) repent and return home.

Some useful interrupters are:

in fact, of course, indeed, I think, without doubt, to be sure, naturally, it seems, after all, for all that, in brief, on the whole, in short, to tell the truth, in any event, clearly, I suppose, I hope, at least, assuredly, certainly, remarkably, importantly, definitely.

Remember the Grammarians call this the Sentential Adverb.

The Neck Bone Connected to...

The Greeks called this Zeugma

In your writing you link several similar words or expressions, with another word or expression.

Examples of this kind of link:

- **one subject with two (or more) verbs:** *Jackie Robinson impressed by his hitting and dazzled by his stealing bases.*
- **a verb with two (or more) direct objects:** *My mother fried* zeppole *and* pignolate.
- **two (or more) subjects with one verb, etc.**
- *Bush and Cheney are responsible for endless war.*

The main benefit of linking expressions like this is that it shows relationships between ideas and actions more clearly.

In one form the linking word goes before the word it links to. For example, you could have a verb clearly stated in the first part of the sentence that links to the idea of the same verb which is understood but not explicitly stated in the words that follow:

Your intelligence will win you honors, your

character admiration.

Fred baked cakes; Mary pies, Tom cookies.

Carlos beat everyone at chess in Buenos Aires and me in New York.

Another form of zeugma links a single subject with multiple verbs:

If you are lucky, your writing will earn you money, impress your peers, and provide you with great satisfaction.

This house had a view of the mountains in front, and faced the prairie out back.

The supervisor glowered angrily, then yelled furiously, and finally walked out sulking.

Sometimes you might want to add attention to your linkage by using the verb in a slightly different sense in the different parts of the statement:

He snatched his coat from the rack and a kiss from his wife.

On the picnic with her boss she fished for trout and for compliments.

Usually two or three links are most common. However, if you want to tell a lot about the subject or if want to show the complexity of its behavior or actions, you can use several verbs:

Whenever he was in Brooklyn, he would crack jokes with Sal, ask Luis to play his guitar, fight with Pete Brown, quote scripture with Mr. Toole, lament the good old days with his mother, talk horses with McGlowry, drink cheap wine with Shapiro, and end up completely out of money but very happy.

You can link two or more subordinate clauses with the noun in question becoming the link:

His father, who was a working man, and who had little love for the pretentious neighbors, always went to community meetings in his work clothes. (The link is "his father")

It is clear speech that communicates best, and that clears the throat most effectively. (The link is "clear speech")

You can link one noun to two or more actions:

With one mighty harrumph he made his point and frightened his listeners.

The farmer grabbed his shovel from the wall, his gloves from the table, and his hat from his wife.

You can link one preposition with two objects:

> *I was charmed by the painter's face and her world- class curves.*

Sometimes for effect, you put the linking word after the words it links together. One common way to do this is with multiple subjects:

> *Hours, days, weeks, months, and years went by.*
> –
> *The students, the faculty, and the parents were all consulted on the new project.*
>
> *To succeed in life and to care for his parents is a Chinese child's code.*
>
> *After the surge and the fires, Rockaway was devastated.*

It is possible also to hold off a verb until the last clause:

> *The little baby in his crib, the old lady in her living room, and the man in his basement workshop, all heard the alarm.*

Linkages can be used with descriptive words too. Here's an example of the linking of two accounts of a person, one past and one present:

> *Failed in love and struggling in business, he was very depressed.*

The utility of Zeugma and other linking devices is that they save repetition of subjects or verbs or other words. They also make evident connections between thoughts. The more connections between ideas you can make in your writing, the clearer it will be.

Remember, the Greeks called this Zeugma

Chapter Three:
Style and Display

Some writers highlight their skill or try to emphasize their message by showing off their style by manipulating the structure, content, o choice of words and phrases.

One way (there are others below) is to begin a sentence in a way that implies a certain logical progression, but end it differently than what is expected from the normal flow of the grammar. For example:

> Bankers that ruin lives of millions, is it right that they go unpunished?

Allusion

Marco Polo would have it a lot easier in today's China

A short, casual reference to some well-known thing or event is an **allusion**. It is very useful in your writing. You count on a common reference point with your reader to make a point without going into detail. An allusion can allow the writer to cast greater notability on their subject without having to resort to outright hyperbole (page 42).

The use of allusions enables writers to simplify complex ideas and emotions. The readers can grasp the complex ideas by comparing the emotions of the writer to the references given by them. References to Greek Mythology give a scholarly or classical tone to the writing. Similarly, biblical allusions may reach religiously oriented readers and listeners.

Since allusions refer to something *other than* what is directly being discussed, your reader may miss an allusion or fail to understand it if they do not have the background you are counting on.

He had a Eureka moment while writing chapter four of his book.

*If I don't put the toilet seat down, I get
World War II all over again.*

He endured the sufferings of Job.

*Hurricane Sandy did the damage of a
modern-day Great Flood.*

*The search for undocumented persons quickly
became a Salem Witch Hunt.*

In these examples the allusions are to very well-
known characters or events, not to obscure ones.
Usually allusions are made to literature, history,
Greek myth, and the Bible.

A very common literary allusion (not familiar to
everyone, so don't overuse it) is to the mythological
labors of Hercules and Alexander.

*To work out the computer program was like
untying a modern Gordian knot.*

*It would take Hercules to clean the stable in
my son's room.*

The purpose of the allusion is to explain or clarify or
emphasize the subject under discussion. The allusion
must be brief so as not to distract the reader.

Allusion can be very attractive in your writing
because it introduces variety and punch into the
discussion.

For example, a romantic allusion might enhance a discussion of chemical compounds.

Water is hydrogen's bigamous relationship with oxygen

The loan shark said, "pay up or I'll break your legs; I'm no Mother Teresa."

This can please the readers by reminding them of a pertinent story or figure with, which can serve as an analogy to explain something difficult. The quick pause and attention to the implied analogy can help the reader to concentrate on the basic material. When used well it shows of the author's breadth of knowledge and can support her credibility.

Remember we call this Allusion

Old Man River, you just keep rollin' along....

The Greeks called this Apostrophe.

When a speaker or writer stops addressing an audience such as a committee or jury in front of her, and addresses <u>directly </u>some other third party that is not present in the original audience, the strategy *apostrophe* is used to show emotion, even by interrupting the train of thought. In older writing this figure was introduced by the exclamation "Oh".

Wikipedia gives us the following classical examples:

> *"Where, my death, is thy sting? where, O death, thy victory?"* **Paul of Tarsus**

> *"Roll on, thou dark and deep blue Ocean — roll!"*
> **Byron, "Childe Harold's Pilgrimage"**

> *"Thou glorious sun!"*
> **Samuel Taylor Coleridge, "This Lime Tree Bower**

> *O books who alone are liberal and free, who give to all who ask of you and enfranchise all who serve you faithfully!*
> **Richard de Bury**

Because it helps memory and learning, apostrophe is

common in nursery rhymes, song lyrics and other forms of popular writing:

> *Twinkle, twinkle, little star, How I wonder what you are.*

> *Shine on, shine on Harvest Moon, up in the sky...*

> *Oh Christmas Tree, oh Christmas Tree...*

In your writing, you might use this device the same way as the Greeks did, to call attention to an emotion, real or feigned.

> Sometimes, surrounded by corrupt politicians, I want to shout, "John Adams, where are you when we need you?"

This device is not used very often in argumentative writing because formal argument is more controlled and intellectual rather than emotional, but in some cases it could be useful.

Although you might not talk this way, using dramatic devices like apostrophe can convey meanings in a more vivid and impressive manner and make speech more effective, attractive, and emphatic.

However, in formal persuasive and informative

writing, using apostrophe might seem forced and distracting."

Remember the Greeks called this Apostrophe

Cry Me A River...
The Greeks called this Catachresis.

An experienced writer can employ overblown metaphors using words in a "wrong", strange or unusual way in order to convey extreme emotion or affectation. This form of communication is difficult to come up with, but when used well, can be very effective.

He looked at the price and his pockets ran dry.
So he grabbed the problem by the horns and decided what to do

I will speak daggers to her. –Hamlet
Or more romantically, *"I will speak flowers to her."*

The writer or speaker replaces the intended meaning with a related idea (as Hamlet did, using *daggers* instead of angry words or *flowers* to communicate loving words):

This device is often considered a vice; however, the ancient rhetorician Quintilian taught that it was legitimate to adapt existing words where an exact word does not exist.

For example, there is no idiom like "sight unseen" for things we hear, so the following idiom could be stretched from its proper context to this unusual one:

He bought the new music CD hearing unheard.

Of course this is a strange use but that is the idea. This particular example may or may not work with you or with all audiences. But the writer may choose to use it as a conceit or *tour de force* to call attention to the underlying meaning of the altered expression. The device may register with some readers with more impact than a merely literal expression.

Similarly, there is no term parallel to "sightseeing" for a descriptive lecture or radio program. A possible adaption of the idea of "seeing" can be made:

The radio program was like a sound-hearing tour of Manhattan.

Nicknames, especially the taunting ones invented by teenagers or workers, fit the original Greek definition of this device called *catachresis*, which includes the idea of abuse.

"elbow nose" for a person with a crooked nose, "football head" for a person with a large head, "pizza face" for a person with acne, "towel head" for a person wearing a turban.

Sometimes you can substitute a noun for a verb or a verb for a noun, a noun for an adjective, and so on.

You should always aim at being effective rather than "corny" or noticeable.

He always goes into a turkey coma on Thanksgiving...

Miss Daisy turtled along at fifteen miles an hour.

She tap-danced her words when she gave her report.

In literature we find these examples:

Or to take arms against a sea of troubles, and, by opposing, end them?
To die, to sleep. **Hamlet by William Shakespeare**

A man that studies revenge keeps his own wounds green.... **On Revenge by Francis Bacon**

Blind mouths!
Milton, Lycidas)

the voice of your eyes is deeper than all roses nobody, not even the rain, has such small hands....
E. E. Cummings

Mow the beard,

Shave the grass,

Pin the plank,

110

Nail my sleeve.
Alexander Pope

Pope comments that the use of this rhetorical device gives us an intellectual pleasure such as that we experience in a circus where the clown shaves with a hatchet but chops down a tree with a razor.

Remember The Greeks called this Catachresis.

Metaphors are the Spice of Writing
The Greeks called this Metaphor.

A metaphor is a figure of speech that identifies one thing as being the same as some unrelated other thing, thus strongly implying the similarities between the two. **Wikipedia**

It is more powerful than a simile. A simile (see 159) compares two items, usually with the word "like", for example, *He roared like a lion.* In contrast, a metaphor directly equates them. *He was a roaring lion,*

The two devices are different in that metaphor makes the point that one thing is another thing, not just that one thing is like another thing, and so does not apply any words of comparison, such as "like" or "as."

Usually, the metaphor stresses the "equality" between two things by using the verb "is".

A mother is the anchor of the family.

A teacher is a beacon of the light of understanding and a fountain of the waters of wisdom.

In the championship game, Caputo was an immovable rock on defense and a roaring lion on offense.

Just as frequently, though, the comparison is clear enough without the verb "is".

My little daughter toddled around the adults' conversation, tape-recording everything of interest to her.

The thought of her lover's treachery put fire in her cheeks and sparks in her eyes.

A teenage boy does not eat; he inhales his food.

His experiences among working people softened his criticisms and hardened his anger against injustice.

The comparison may or not be explicitly expressed.

Your attitude illuminates your body; when it is cheerful, your eyes and your whole body are full of light; but when it is grumpy, even your skin and hair look dark and dull.

In this case the comparison, the attitude is a source of light or a lamp, is declared <u>directly</u>, and the points of similarity are spelled out.

But in the following examples the comparison is

113

<u>not</u> <u>directly stated.</u>

Look at this *piropo* (flirtatious compliment) said to a young woman in a green dress:

> *Wow! If this is the bud, what will the flower be like?*

Here the unstated comparison is between something like "adolescence" or "youth" and "full maturity" So the rhetorical question is, "If you're so beautiful now, what will you look like at your peak?"

> *Go and tell that rat, "I will do what I have to do and then I will go for him."*

It is understood that the enemy is considered a rat.

> *It's raining cats and dogs.*

It's not sure what the reference is; maybe it is the idea of a chaotic amount, like a jumble of cats and dogs. But we get the idea.

The ancient grammarians teach us that when there is a great difference between the two parts of the comparison, the subject should always be compared to something greater or more notable. If not, the comparison will fail. You might write, "The electric light in the dark basement was the prisoner's sun", but you wouldn't write, "The sun on a clear day is a big electric bulb."

> *For thou hast been my help, and in the*

shadow of thy wings I sing for joy. **Psalm 63:7**

Here, the writer wants to convey a sense of tenderness and protection, so he draws on a familiar image, that of a hen and her chicks. Here, the comparison, "God is a bird [or hen]" is only implied. Stating the equation directly would not work because of the awkward thought it would bring to mind. The author gets across the idea of concern and protection by evoking the image of a hen with her chicks under her wings.

Like simile and analogy, metaphor is an extremely valuable and useful device. Aristotle says in his *Rhetoric*, "It is metaphor above all else that gives clearness, charm, and distinction."

By these direct comparisons and indirect allusions certain aspects or characteristics are grasped by the imagination which enable us to see something like the "color and shape" of these features. This gives the reader a great deal of satisfaction, as well as helping the understanding.

In this way, a metaphor not only explains by making an abstract or unknown idea concrete and familiar, but it also pleases by stirring the reader's imagination.

Metaphor, by laying bare the relationship between alien things, opens our minds to the philosophical idea of the interconnection in the unity of all things.

115

The fact that two very unlike things have something in common or can be described or referred to in terms of one another says something about both of them. No metaphor is "just a metaphor." Every metaphor has significant implications. The writer must choose carefully because the comparison may evoke non-intended ideas. Look at the differences in meaning suggested by these statements:

- *There are new ideas that are spreading like wildfire.*
- *There are new ideas that are spreading like cancer.*
- *There are new ideas that are really blossoming now.*
- *There are new ideas that are engulfing the campus.*

Remember that the metaphor is so impactful and communicative that it is sometimes understood literally rather than as a comparison. You, like all writers, must be careful in your writing to avoid possible confusion.

Metaphor is often confused with other figures of speech which are similar but not the same, synechdoche (page 165) and metonymy (page 123), which is a common way of indicating relationship by substituting a part for the whole, or the whole for the part. For example, to call your car "my wheels" is a synecdoche. A part of the car, its "wheels" stands for the whole car.

In a metonymy, on the other hand, the word we use to describe a thing is closely linked to the thing, but is not a part of it. For example, "PULL", which means power or influence, is a metonymy in the expression "He has pull with the boss".

Metonymy is different from a metaphor which points out the similarity between two different things as in "Joe is a time bomb". A person and a bomb are two different things but the metaphor describes Joe as a bomb based on a supposed similarity (maybe his outbursts of anger, his impatience, etc.)

Remember the Greeks called this Metaphor.

The Redcoats Are Coming!
The Greeks called this Metonymy.

ॐ

This is a figure of speech that replaces the name of one thing with the name of another with which it is closely associated. We find examples of metonymy both in literature and in everyday expressions.

Just like with other literary devices, a metonymy adds interest to the writing. Instead of repeating, "the principal officers of the department" every time you want to refer to the organization, one word "the brass" communicates your idea...

Economy of words is not the only reason for using a metonymy; it also serves purpose of changing the flow of the wording to make the sentence more interesting.

Metonymy is used frequently in everyday life. To understand it better, here a few more examples of metonymy:

Mexico decides to control emigration.
("Mexico" refers to the government.)

The suits entered the meeting with the union.
("Suits" commonly stand for managers.)

The pen is mightier than the sword. **("Pen" and "sword" refer to written words and military force.)**

The Oval Office is crowded with lobbyists. **("The Oval Office" is a metonymy which stands for the Presidency of the United States.)**

Give her a hand! **("Hand" means help.)**

Metonymy Examples from Literature

"Friends, Romans, countrymen, lend me your ears." **Julius Caesar "Ears" stands for attention.**

"I'm mighty glad Georgia waited till after Christmas before it seceded or it would have ruined the Christmas parties." **Gone with the Wind. "Georgia" is State Government.**

Metonymy is often confused with two figures of speech which are similar but not the same, metaphor (page 117) and synecdoche (page 165)

Synecdoche is a common way of indicating relationship by substituting a part for the whole, or the whole for the part. For example, to call your car "my wheels" is a synecdoche. A part of the car, its "wheels" stands for the whole car.

Metonymy on the other hand is different from a metaphor which points out the similarity between two different things as in "Joe is a time bomb". We just saw the metaphor which paints Joe as a bomb due to a supposed similarity.

In a metonymy, on the other hand, the word we use to describe a thing is closely linked to the thing, but is not a part of it. For example, "pull", which means power or influence, is a metonymy in the expression "He has pull with the boss".

Metonymy builds on close associations and helps the writer to exhibit deeper or hidden meanings. It also lends to conciseness as in "City Hall is raising taxes". *City Hall here stands for city government.*

In summary, metonymy, like other rhetorical and literary devices, is used to bring words to life. Simple things and ideas are described creatively way to this bring "life" to the thoughts presented.

Remember the Greeks called this Metonymy.

Your Face is Killing Me!

The Ancients called this Personification.

One device to make your writing more interesting is by to give human qualities to an animal or thing. In other words, you make them act like people or "persons" in your writing. That is why this device is called "Personification". You metaphorically endow the animal, inanimate object, or idea with personality. That is, you make the thing a person.

> *The truck groaned and complained under the extra weight.*
>
> *This house is more friendly than the other one.*
>
> *I can't fix this car because this bolt refuses to let go. Peggy heard the last piece of cheesecake in the refrigerator calling her name.*
>
> *He sang a lonely song to the moonlight.*
>
> *The thunder gave the order and the raindrops reported for duty.*
>
> *The sunflowers nodded in the wind.*
>
> *The angry storm pounded on the tin roof. New York, the city that never sleeps.*

The trees dropped their leaves and rested. I overheard the streets talking about you. Winter's icy grip squeezed his rib cage.

A case of cupcakes can charm an empty stomach.

December light is brief and uncharitable.

This morning had friendly greetings for peaceful sleepers.

The party died as soon as she left. Light had conquered darkness.

My neighbor's cat preened as arrogantly and haughtily as any aristocrat.

It is not only things that can be personified. A writer can also personify ideas or concepts.

Wisdom cries aloud in the streets; in the markets she raises her voice. **Psalm 1:20**

Death, where is thy sting? **1 Corinthians 15:55**

The rhetorical device of Personification is used mostly for artistic effect to create a pleasing intellectual appreciation of the view of the writer or speaker. But it also can serve clarity and understanding by making abstractions clearer and more real to the reader or listener by defining or explaining a concept in terms of everyday human activity, thus bringing ideas to life.

But be careful of being corny or trite. Personification is a powerful way to express your view of things, but avoid overused expressions such as "winking stars", or "wailing ambulances".

The reader does not receive much pleasure from an overdone expression like the following:

> *The angry tree in the hateful forest cruelly shook down its hateful drops upon the poor man...*

Nevertheless, putting a human face on a cold abstraction or natural phenomenon helps us to understand it, and to organize the world on our own terms, so that we can communicate it better. For example in the following example, the writer sees his own feelings in the inanimate world around him:

> *After two hours of long sentences broken only by silly jokes, everyone was bored. The members were bored; the audience was bored; the lecturer herself was bored. Even the chairs were bored.*

Remember the Ancients called this Personification.

Beat Them To The Punch

The Greeks called this Procatalepsis.

A handy device in your writing is to anticipate an objection and then answer it. This lets you progress towards making your point while clearing away arguments that are contrary to your final conclusions. Often the objections are trivial ones:

> *Some people say that recycling is too expensive. It is true that up-front costs will be necessary but the growing revenue stream from the materials sold will recoup the expenses incurred. Furthermore, we cannot skimp on spending money to save the planet.*

> *Politicians all over are railing against "Social Promotion", the practice of moving failing students on to the next grade. They say that failure should not be rewarded. This puritanical punitive view of a child's development sits well with middle class voters. Nevertheless, research shows that students who are left back to repeat a grade consistently do worse than those that are kept with their classmates.*

Sometimes the writer himself will present negative scenarios in order to show how to solve them.

However, only a weak writer will bring forward obviously weak arguments.

> But what if a young person decides not to go to college? Although in most cases, this will affect her lifetime earnings, it is not always an error for all students. A skilled technician or business owner may do better in life both economically and emotionally, than a run of the mill cubicle-dwelling college graduate.

Differences of education, of culture, or of command of language all affect your readers' understanding of what you write. You may have to address these issues before going into your argument.

> The preacher says, "You can have a better life". You say, "How, with my lousy job?" The preacher says, "Many before you have worked and bettered themselves."

> In your country you are used to having your daughters drop in to say hello, or to occasionally bring you a special dish. Don't always expect this from your children raised in the United States where it is considered a value for new families to be independent.

Conservatives say that too much tax money is spent on food stamps; they point to cases of abuse and corruption. Sure, I concede that the system is not perfect. I share with them a desire to eliminate as many ills as possible. But I do not lose sight of the fact that a hungry child is an abomination.

If you bring up objections to your argument, you show that you are aware of them and can respond to them. If you avoid the objections to your case, you may appear ignorant or dishonest.

Some words to get into using this valuable literary device could be:

Some people wonder...
Don't get this wrong...
Be sure you understand...
You may be thinking...
Maybe you don't understand the main idea...

Remember, the Greeks called this Procatalepsis.

Stop, go away, that's enough rhetoric!

The Greeks called this Pleonasm

Some writers purposely use more words than required to express an idea; this is usually a bad idea, but can be done on purpose for literary effect or for accentuation:

It used to be common in legal writing to express the same thought in different terms supposedly to ensure the clear understanding of the main points of the argument:

> *The judge ordered the builders to cease and desist.*

> *Jones assigns, grants, transfers, conveys, and alienates his interest to Smith.*

> *His home, residence, and domicile is in Texas.*

> *After the settlement, the rest, residue, and remainder go to the children.*

> *The deceased had been advised to give, devise, and bequeath all her estate to charity.*

However, this use of pleonasm in legal writing is fast disappearing in favor of clearer writing. Nevertheless, the use of the tactic might still be useful in your writing for impact and effect.

We heard it with our own ears.

That statement is wrong, incorrect, and not true at all in any way, shape, or form.

Nothing, zero, zilch, nada!

The director told the staff to collect the material, get organized, and to tie up the loose ends.

He is a hardworking, conscientious, cooperative employee.

"These terrible things I have seen with my own eyes, and I have heard with my own ears, and touched with my own hands."
Isabel Allende, City of the Beasts.

I will give it to you free, gratis, and for nothing.

"This was the most unkindest cut of all."
William Shakespeare, Julius Caesar.

Pleonasms can also be useful for more than emphasizing the meaning of the words. They can help to loosen up the rhythm of your writing. For example, if your writing or speech is too constricted or terse, readers may find it lacks ease or grace.

If you edit your writing too tightly you make it seem artificial, stilted or awkward, especially if words are cut from well-known ways of phrasing things. The use of pleonasm can make it lighter, more flexible and fluid.

On the other hand, as with any use of language, excessive repetition of expressions weakens writing and speech.

Unnecessary words distract from the content. William Strunk Jr. advocated the right balance in The Elements of Style (1918):

> *"Vigorous writing is concise. A sentence should contain no unnecessary words, a paragraph no unnecessary sentences, for the same reason that a drawing should have no unnecessary lines and a machine no unnecessary parts. This requires not that the writer make all his sentences short, or that he avoid all detail and treat his subjects only in outline, but that every word tell."*

Remember, the Greeks called this Pleonasm

One potato, two potato...

The Greeks called this Anaphora

Often the repetition of the same word or words at the beginning of successive phrases, clauses, or sentences will add interest and strength to the presentation of your thoughts. Often repetition is used together with climax and with parallelism. See page 89 for climax and page 77 for parallelism.)

> *A good mother gets obedience without spanking, without angry words, without bribes and toys.*

> *If we can get the car started, if we can find the right road, and if we can see the sign for the turn off, we should get there by midnight.*

> *Not wanting food, not wanting drink, not wanting human contact, the poor man was resigned to a lonely death.*

> *In books I find the dead as if they were alive; in books I foresee things to come; in books warlike affairs are set forth; from books come forth the laws of peace.* **Richard de Bury**

Some modern examples are:

To be a writer, you must have a broad strategy: instead of trying to impress your readers with involved logic, you must hope to improve them; instead of looking for praise for clever turns of phrase, you should aim at fame by the depth of your content.

Modern corporate mass media provide entertainment to people with no ideas of their own and therefore easily prey to influences; with no firm principles and therefore easily following the latest fad; with no personal experience and therefore open to every false argument and reasoning.

It's the hope of slaves sitting around a fire singing freedom songs; the hope of immigrants setting out for distant shores; the hope of a young naval lieutenant bravely patrolling the Mekong Delta; the hope of a millworker's son who dares to defy the odds; the hope of a skinny kid with a funny name who believes that America has a place for him, too.
Barack Obama, "The Audacity of Hope

"We shall go on to the end, we shall fight in France, we shall fight on the seas and oceans, we shall fight with growing confidence and

131

*growing strength in the air, we shall defend
our Island, whatever the cost may be, we shall
fight on the beaches, we shall fight on the
landing grounds, we shall fight in the fields
and in the streets, we shall fight in the hills; we
shall never surrender.* **Winston Churchill, June 4,
1940**

*Five fish caught,
Five hours in the sun, and
Five dollars for bus fare... What a failure!"*

*May the road rise up to meet you.
May the wind always be at your back.*

*May the sun shine warm upon your
face, and rains fall soft upon your
fields.*

*And until we meet again, May God hold you in
the palm of His hand.*
Irish Blessing

An equally spiritual example:
*But one hundred years later, the Negro still is
not free. One hundred years later, the life of
the Negro is still sadly crippled by the
manacles of segregation and the chains of
discrimination. One hundred years later, the
Negro lives on a lonely island of poverty in
the midst of a vast ocean of material
prosperity. One hundred years later, the*

Negro is still languishing in the corners of American society and finds himself an exile in his own land. And so we've come here today to dramatize a shameful condition. "
Dr. Martin Luther King, Jr., "I Have a Dream," 1963

You see that Anaphora is the repetition of the same phrase or word at the <u>beginning</u> of successive sentences.

But, in epistrophe (page 146) the same or related phrases or words are repeated at the <u>end</u> of successive sentences, for example:

I scream, you scream, we all scream for ice cream

This device can be used with questions, denials, opinions, conclusions, and subordinating conjunctions, adverbs and prepositions although care must be taken not to appear false or forced in your use of it.

Remember, the Greeks called this Anaphora

Give it a good think!

Anthimeria: uses a word in a way that obliges the reader understand it as a different part of speech.

A noun can be used as a verb or a verb as an adjective. This is possible in English, but not in all languages. Shakespeare was very imaginative and playful with this writing trick.

> *The thunder would not peace at my bidding.*
> **King Lear**
> The noun *peace* is used as a verb.

> *"I'll unhair thy head."* **Antony and Cleopatra**
> The noun *hair* is used as a verb.

> *And thus the native hue of resolution*
> *Is sicklied o'er with the pale cast of thought.*
> **Hamlet**

But it not only Shakespeare who uses this device. Sometimes we use it when we can't think of an appropriate word so we invent one based on another which usually is used differently. The ability to do this is a powerful tool for the writer and speaker of English. Here are some examples in less "literary" writing.

The bright sun in the windows summered *the cold room.*

The car fishtailed *on the icy road.*

The hungry teenagers had eat *written all over their faces.*

This use of words is so natural to English that often we don't notice the origin of many verbs made from nouns:

> He *ramrodded* the bill through Congress.
>
> The fullback *stiff-armed* the tackler.
>
> The prosecutor *railroaded* the accused man.
>
> The sailors were *shanghaied.*
>
> Our line *defensed* their heart out at the goal line.
>
> Sometimes the best remedy is a good *cry.*

This device is not only effective; you will find it to be a lot of fun. You get the chance to juggle the words in your writing just as you feel like. It is not only a question of putting your personal stamp on our writing; in some cases you will actually improve the English language with new uses for old words.

Remember, the Greeks called this *Anthimeria.*

The Caboose of the Phrase

The Greeks called this Epistrophe

As you saw above, repetition will be a valuable tool in your writing. There is another related device for you to use. You can repeat the same word or words at the end of successive phrases, clauses, or sentences. We might call it a Wrap-up Repetition This is a very powerful device because of the special force that comes with the last word in a phrase or sentence.

Where lobbyists are abundant, independent legislators are scarce; where police surveillance is excessive, civil liberties are scarce; where money rules, democracy is scarce.

You will have to read to pass this course; you will have to write to pass this course, and most of all you will have to think to pass this course.

For no government is better than the men who compose it, and I want the best, *and we need* the best, *and we deserve* the best.
Senator John F. Kennedy, Oct. 17, 1960

"Who is here so base that would be a bondman? If any, speak; for him have I offended. Who is

136

here so rude that would not be a Roman? If any,
speak; for him have I offended. Who is here so
vile that will not love his country? If any, speak;
for him have I offended....Julius Caesar, **William**
Shakespeare

"When I was a child, I spoke as a child, I
understood as a child, I thought as a child".
Paul, of Tarsus: Corinthians 13:11

Epistrophe is the repetition of the same phrase or word at the end of successive sentences.

Anaphora (already seen in this collection on page 140) is the repetition of the same phrase or word at the beginning of successive sentences.

Five fish caught,
Five hours in the sun, and
Five dollars for bus fare... What a failure!

The truth, the whole truth, and nothing but the truth

If you have an idea you want to stress heavily, then this device of repeating the idea at the end of a phrase might be a good construction to use. The danger as in all the rhetorical devices featured in this book, is in overusing this tool.

Remember, the Greeks called this Epistrophe

Daisy Chain

The Greeks called this Anadiplosis

Repetition as seen in the previous device is a useful device that can add, underline or emphasize the logic of your writing. You can go even further by repeating the last word or concept of one part of your expression at the beginning of the following part.

It is used to underline the repeated word or idea and reinforces the writer's argument.

> *His strong point is his intelligence and it is his intelligence that gets him in trouble.*

> *How much confidence can we have in a leader, when this leader denies the reality of climate change?*

> *"I am Sam; Sam I am."* Dr. Seuss, Green Eggs and Ham

> *This car has excellent popularity, popularity that ensures its resale value.*

> *We get health through good food and we get good food through good governmental regulation.*

In the beginning was the Word, and the Word was with God, and the Word was God. John 1:1

With this device the main point of the sentence becomes clear. By repeating the same word twice in close succession, you emphasize the focus of your thought when you use it.

You can use also this tool to create a sequence to emphasize a logical progression:

> *A good person studies to be wise, uses her wisdom to be strong, uses her strength to serve others, and her service strengthens those she serves.*

Remember, the Greeks called this Anadiplosis

Play it Again, Sam
The Romans called this Conduplicatio

❧

Another useful tool is the repetition of a preceding key word (not just the last word) from a preceding phrase, clause, or sentence, at the beginning of the next.

"Where have all the flowers gone? Long time passing.

Where have all the flowers gone? Long time ago.

Where have all the flowers gone?

Girls have picked them every one. When will they ever learn?

When will they ever learn?"
(Pete Seeger and Joe Hickerson)

It was not often that anger influenced his actions. But anger eventually caused his downfall.

The heat of the chili peppers is no excuse for panting and moaning. True gourmets enjoy the heat as part of the dining experience.

It is acceptable to look for wealth as a means to personal growth; to seek wealth for itself is shameful.

I could list the problems which cause people to feel cynical, problems which include lack of integrity in government, the feeling that the individual no longer counts...
Barbara Jordan, 1976

"Blessed are the poor in spirit: for theirs is the kingdom of heaven.

Blessed are they that mourn: for they shall be comforted.

Blessed are the meek: for they shall inherit the earth.

Blessed are they that hunger and thirst after righteousness: for they shall be filled.

Blessed are the merciful: for they shall obtain mercy.

Blessed are the pure in heart: for they shall see God.

Blessed are the peacemakers: for they shall be called sons of God.

Blessed are they that have been persecuted for righteousness' sake: for theirs is the kingdom of heaven." **Jesus, Sermon on the Mount, Matthew 5:3-10**

Like the other repetitive device of above, doubling serves as an effective way to focus your argument because with it, you can pull out a key idea from the preceding sentence and put it clearly at the beginning of the new sentence, leading the reader towards what he or she should concentrate on.

Since good writing implies keeping the reader focused on a thread of thought, this tool can be especially helpful to clarify the writer's intention when the first sentence has two or more possible main points, only one of which the writer wants to stress. For example, if your first sentence is complex, such as the following, the conduplicatio device will help communicate your ideas clearly.

> *The election of judges by a popular vote in a regular election has the danger that both the campaign and the people's choice could be based on popularity with special interests and not on the personal assets and qualifications of the best candidate... (A next clause could come in here)*

In the above example, to keep the ideas clear, the next clause could be either of these two following sentences depending on which concept you wish to develop.

Either,

> *because special interests which are the*

nemesis of Democracy could influence a popular vote.

Or,

therefore, the best candidate is often unknown to the voting public in a popular vote, and judges might be better selected by the executive branch.

This repetition of the idea in which the writer is most interested helps the reader focus on this idea which is carried forward and developed in the second sentence.

Remember, the Romans called this Conduplicatio

That's how it is!

The Greeks called this Metabasis.

ઈ∾

This communication device consists of a brief transitional statement of what has been said and what will follow

Good writers summarize often to keep the reader in touch with the point of view of the writing. A summary in different parts of the writing links thoughts and maintains order in their progressive presentation:

> *So far in this meeting everyone has been concentrating on the difficulties we face. I want to lay out for you the strong points of our position.*
>
> *Up to now I have looked at Smith's proposal only in terms of finances. This background was necessary for us to go on and consider the legal aspects of the proposal.*

A brief summary throughout your writing helps your reader to appreciate, organize, and remember your argument.

For example, using a summary helps to link different sections of your views, and lets you direct the reader's attention to related topics or to other material dependent on the current matter.

> *Now that I have told you about the kinship patterns of the Inuit, let me go on to describe some family interactions.*

A summary can also bring together large sections of preceding material:

> *The previous sections of this work show the complexity of the English language. There was a discussion of the underlying Germanic grammar, as well as examples of Saxon and Celtic vocabulary.*

> *Finally, we treated the large impact of Norman French and academic Latin on the present state of the language.*

Many writers on rhetorical devices quote J.G. Smith on this device.

Smith (quoted in *"Silva Rhetoricae"* Gideon O. Burton) lists eight kinds of metabasis, according to the kind of connection that is found between the earlier and later content:

1. Equal
The matters you have heard were wonderful, and those that you shall hear are no less marvelous.

2. Unequal
You have heard very grievous things, but you shall hear more grievous.

3. Like
I have spoken of his notable enterprises in France, and now I will rehearse his worthy acts done in England.

4. Contrary
As I have spoken of his sad adversity and misery, so will I now speak of his happy prosperity.

5. Differing
I have spoken of manners; now it remains that I speak concerning doctrine.

6. Anticipating Objection
You may think me too long in the threatening of the law; I will now pass to the sweet promises of the gospel.

7. Reprehension
Why do I dwell on these things? I shall hasten my speech unto that which is the principal point of the matter in question.

8. Consequences
You have heard how he promised, and now I will tell you how he performed.

9. Related Figures

This device is most useful in longer works. A short piece will not have great need of summarizing.

However, it still is useful to signal relations and links in your writing however short it may be, by using words that guide the reader, such as: *now, next, additionally, further, besides,* etc.

Remember, the Greeks called this Metabasis.

Life is like a box of Chocolates

The Romans called this Simile.

Ok, this section is headed by Forrest Gumps's folksy simile. But you get the idea. A simile is a comparison between two different things that resemble each other in some way.

This device is used for comparing an unfamiliar thing to some familiar thing (an object, event, process, etc.) known to the reader. You can use the simile as a tool for clarifying an idea or concept, but often it is used to make an impression, as an example of cleverness, artistic or poetic style in your writing.

Usually, and especially when a noun is compared with a noun, the simile is usually introduced by the word *like*:

> *"... her frail soul, tormenting itself in its invincible ignorance like a small bird beating about the cruel wires of a cage.*
> **Joseph Conrad, Lord Jim**

An anguished person in jail is like a bird in a cage.

> After too long in the direct sun, my mother in law *looked like a piece of overcooked bacon.*

Many times the simile, the object that is being compared to, precedes the thing compared to it. In these cases, the word *"so"* is used to show the comparison:

> *The grass bends with the wind; so does the typical politician.*

> *A quiet stream runs deep, so does the thoughtful person.*

But sometimes the word *so* is understood rather than expressed:

> *"I wandered lonely as a cloud*
> *that floats on high o'er vales and hills."*
> **Daffodils, William Wordsworth**

> *"Shall I compare thee to a summer's day? Thou art more lovely and more temperate"* **William Shakespeare, Sonnet 18**

> *As wax melts before the fire, may the wicked perish before God.* **Psalm 68**

Sometimes, as in the example given at the beginning of this chapter, *an anguished person in jail is like a bird in a cage,* the comparison is clear.

Whenever it is not immediately clear to the reader what is the point of similarity between the unlike objects, A good writer has to specify the comparison to avoid confusion and vagueness. For example, it is not enough to say,

A good name is like glass
On my job, I am like a mushroom.
She felt like a melon at the vegetable market.

To make the writer's point more information about the comparison is needed.

A good name is like glass, — the brighter the shine, the more easily it can shatter.

"On my job, I am like a mushroom. They keep me in the dark and feed me shit."

She felt like a melon at the vegetable market; she had been poked and squeezed so much that no one picked her up.

Often the point of similarity can be expressed in just a word or two, with no explanation.

He is as useless as tits on a bull.
Yes, he is a cute puppy, but he will be as big as a house.

Sometimes, the simile word can be used as an adjective:

He uses weasel words and slippery arguments.

His speech had a drum-like monotony to it.

Similes can also be negative, making the point that

two things are unlike in one or more respects:

> *His artwork isn't like a blinding light but it does have its charm.*

> *I wouldn't say he fought like a tiger, but he possessed a quiet tenaciousness as he worked towards his goals.*

Other ways to use similes include the use of comparison:

Ramiro ran around searching for an apartment more than a squirrel searching for acorns in the fall.

But this truth is clearer than spring water.

So a variety of ways exists for invoking the simile. Here are a few of the possibilities:

> *Butter is like margarine.*

> *Butter is not like margarine.*

> *Butter is the same as margarine.*

> *Butter is better than margarine.*

> *Butter is similar to margarine.*

> *Butter   resembles margarine.*

But a simile can sometimes be implied. In such cases no comparative word is needed:

How could I describe my English teacher?
She had thousands of quotations memorized
but could never fit them into a conversation.

When I think of the ACT exam, I think of
slavery and torture and evil professors.

Leslie has the hair and skin of a model...

Some grammarians used to insist that when a verb or phrase is compared to a verb or phrase, the word *as* must be used.

They kept focused on their goal, as a
sunflower always turns to the sun.

Here is your big chance. You have to run as
a person running for his life.

However, this now sounds a little forced and no longer is used. Usually the word *like* is acceptable. This was once a big issue with the commercial for a cigarette brand: *"Winston tastes good like a cigarette should."*

Despite the academic complaints no one thought it was normal speech to say, "Winston tastes good as a cigarette should."

Nowadays, most persons would say that both of the previous sentences could be correct, as well as the following:

They focus on their goal, like a sunflower always turns to the sun.

Here is your big chance. You have to run like a person running for his life.

Remember the Romans called this Simile.

He's the brains of the outfit

The Greeks called this Synecdoche.

ॐ

A common way to compare things is to substitute a part for the whole, or the whole for the part. This trick makes the group stand for a member of the group, or substitutes a member for the group, the material for the thing made, etc.

> *It's hard to make a dollar.*
>
> *The scoundrel chased all the skirts.*
>
> *Hey, Army, where did you get that girl?*
>
> *The firefighter is the city's insurance policy.*
>
> *The workers railed against management.*
>
> *Capital trumps the public's rights.*

So, we use this tool to make any part of anything to stand for the whole thing. Also we can refer to the thing itself to refer to any part of the whole.

> *The farmer has five hundred head of cattle and three hired hands.*

It is clear that the rancher also owns the bodies of the cattle, and that the hired hands show up for work with

154

their bodies attached. This is a simple part-for-whole example.

Make sure to make your metaphor clear by using a central and obvious part to represent the whole.

> *I wish I had some wheels to get to work.*

> We understand that you also need to get the rest of the car.

And notice the other kinds of substitutions that can be made:

> *With Mozart on the record player I relaxed in my room*

> I hope he doesn't get dizzy spinning around! The composer stands for the record.

> *If you want, you can use plastic.*

> That is, if you have funds! The credit card is represented by the material it is made of.

> *Babe Ruth was the Wizard of Wood.*

> The material represents the bat that Babe Ruth used to hit the baseball.

One common way to use this device is to substitute genus for species, that is, you choose the class to which the idea or thing to be expressed belongs, instead of the idea or thing itself:

My transportation is in the garage.

However, the following example shows a possible problem

The missile went toward the opponents.

Confusion can arise when we use a general term to stand for a more specific term (the class for the member). In the example above some more information is needed to clarify that "missile" means "rock" in this case, rather than, say, "ballistic" or "guided" missile. Usually the context is enough to keep things clear but you must be aware of the possible confusion.

It is easier to understand (but not mandatory) to make something specific refer to something more general, that is to make a single, specific, representative item stand for the whole. This will usually be clearer and more effective:

Life depends on more than cars and television sets.
Two specific things stand for material wealth.

Give us this day our daily bread. Matt. 6:11
Bread standing for complete physical well-being.

Our party stands for "Joe Six-Pack".

A nickname representing a whole class of people.

The orders came directly from the City Hall.
Here we know that the writer means the Mayor gave the orders, because "City Hall" makes us think of "Mayor".

Wow, it's hot. The mercury is rising like crazy.

Of course, "mercury" stands for the temperature

Synecdoche is often confused with two other figures of speech which are similar but not the same, metaphor (page 117), and metonymy (page 123).

A *metaphor* points out the similarity between two different things as in "Joe is a time bomb". A person and a bomb are two different things but the metaphor describes Joe as a bomb based on a supposed similarity (maybe his outbursts of anger, his impatience, etc.)

In a *metonymy*, on the other hand, the word we use to describe a thing is closely linked to that thing but is not a part of it. For example, "pull", which means power or influence, is a metonymy in the expression "He has pull with the boss". Metonymy builds on close associations as in "City Hall is raising taxes".

City Hall here represents the people who work in it.

Get used to using these nuances of language, and you will get the desired effects of connotation, suggestion, and substitution in your writing

Remember The Greeks called this Synecdoche.

My Way or the Highway
The Romans called this Assonance and so do we

The repetition of identical or similar <u>vowel </u>sounds in neighboring words.

Hear the mellow wedding bells
Edgar Allen Poe

The silly pig sat on the fat cat
Children's' rhyme

Try to light the fire
I need to feed the geese.

Just like many of the other literary device, assonance also has a very key role to play in both poetry and prose.

Writers can use it to enhance a musical or rhythmic effect in the text to create internal rhyme, which can heighten the pleasure of reading a literary piece

Assonance differs from alliteration (page 177), which repeats <u>consonant </u>sounds. It also differs from rhyme which calls attention to both vowel and consonant sounds.

Two-word assonance which calls attention to the phrase and helps the reader remember it, is useful for effect as well as for style. However, often the vowels of several words not next to each other are repeated; this causes a pleasing artistic effect.

The different vowel sounds have a different effect on the reader or listener. . Assonance helps writers to develop a particular mood in the text that corresponds with its subject matter.

The "long vowels" sound like the name of the letter in the alphabet. For example, The words "make", "pie", and "go" have long vowels which sound like the names of the letter "a", "i", and "o". Long vowels are heavy and can make a piece more grave and somber. They slow down the pace of the writing. The effect of the long vowel sounds is not always easy to note. You may not sense any effect in the following selections. If this is your reaction, try to read them slowly out loud.

Dylan Thomas uses the long "o" and the long "a" to evoke the fear of death.

> *Do not go gentle into that good night,*
> *Old age should burn and rave at close of day;*
> *Rage, rage, against the dying of the light. . . .*
> *Grave men, near death, who see with blinding*
> *sight Blind eyes could blaze like meteors and be*
> *gay, Rage, rage against the dying of the light.*

In the following example by Carl Sandburg, in *Early Moon*, the long "o" stresses the old and mysterious.

"Poetry is old, ancient, goes back far. It is among the oldest of living things. So old it is that no man knows how and why the first poems came." **Carl Sandburg**

On the other hand high sounds ("short vowels" like those of "sat", "bet", "book", etc.) communicate more vitality:

Let's sing a song
As we tread the path
Of all that is good and best

"Strips of tinfoil winking like people" - **Sylvia Plath**

Don't forget that assonance, like other similar sonorous poetry devices, alliteration, and consonance, can call too much attention in prose and should be used with care.

Just like alliteration has found a place in advertising, assonance also is used to make us remember a product:

"It beats as it sweeps as it cleans!"
"Blue Moon Foods"
"The Cookbook Nook"

The Romans called this assonance, and so do we

Mister Clean

The Greeks called this Epithet.

❧

Sometimes there is one word that really sums up what a person, place or thing is. It is *the* perfect word. That perfect word is an epithet. It can be an adjective or adjective phrase that names a key or important characteristic of the person, place or thing, as in *"Rocket Man","Fat Albert", "New York, the City that Never Sleeps", "utter contempt," The Come-back Kid", "peaceful sleep," "bright dawn,"* etc.

At its simplest, an epithet is merely an adjective, a phrase, or any word that tells us something more about another word. But sometimes it is a little more. You can use a metaphorical epithet, as in "lazy afternoon," "smug landscape," "shouting billboards," "seductive apple."

Clarity and punch are key in choosing epithets. Be original; look for striking images. Strong epithets often have elements of metaphor (page 117) and allusion (page 107

Sometimes the epithet is an adjective applied to a noun which it does not usually describe, but which works in a figurative sense:

The poor woman let out a ragged scream.

Blind mouths of politicians that don't denounce the ills of their cities.

In an age of cybernetic happiness, we sometimes lose the joys of intimacy.

This kind of figurative epithet calls attention to the point made, and can therefore be used to introduce emphatically a new idea. The phrase remains with the reader, so there is no need to repeat it, which would make it obvious and annoying. For example, if you introduce the phrase, "diluted intelligence", it is more forceful not to repeat it but to continue with more normal expressions and synonyms, such as low IQ, inability to grasp, lower percentile, etc.

Also it is better to save your epithet for the end of your argument where it will be clearer and will serve as a summary and synonym for the points you have made, a kind of final wrap-up of the issue.

Epithets are often used in politics. President H.W. Bush, although a decorated war hero, was plagued by the epithet "wimp" put on him by his opponents.

Small minded people use racial or ethnic slurs and labels as derogatory epithets.

You will never use such reprehensible tactics in your writing but you can repeat epithets based on some real characteristic of a person as a means to keep your listeners' and readers' attention on the basis for the label.

An epithet can have the goal of bringing out virtues faults in a person, such as "flip-flop Mike" to indicate a person's indecisiveness, or the constancy of "Steady Eddie".

Sometimes the same epithet can be used as a negative or a positive allusion according to the history of the person and current opinion, such as "Speedy Gonzalez" or "Nick the Quick". The writer may be alluding to either their speed in finishing a job, or to their rushed and shoddy work.

Remember the Greeks called this Epithet.

Method to my Madness.

The Romans called this Alliteration, so do we.

Literary devices are used to produce a pleasing effect in our speaking or writing. Some devices play with the flow and organization of the ideas, some with the sound of the spoken words.

One such device is assonance, mentioned on page 170, which repeats a vowel sound in a phrase or sentence.

Now we'll look at Alliteration, another literary device by which the writer purposely starts two or more consecutive words (or nearby words) with the same consonant <u>sound,</u> not with the same <u>letter</u>. So "new knife" is alliterative, but "kitchen knife" is not. It is often used in poetry, literature, slogans, and other propaganda because it is noticeable and can be easily remembered.

> *That editorial is a piece of pernicious prose.*

> *For a new intern to find favor is a satisfying sensation.*

Alliteration plays an obvious role in poetry and other literature. It creates a musical effect in the text which increases the reading and recitation pleasure. This makes easier to appreciate. It also gives flow and beauty to a piece of writing.

> *"The fair breeze blew, the white foam flew, the furrow followed free;* Coleridge, the Ancient Mariner

> *"The day to cheer and night's dank dew to dry,*
> Romeo and Juliet

> *"In a summer season, when soft was the sun,*
> Piers Plowman, 14 century England

Alliteration calls attention to the phrase, helps the reader remember it, and is useful for effect as well as for style. However, often several words not next to each other are alliterated; this causes a pleasing artistic effect.

> *Do not let such evils overwhelm you as thousands have suffered, and thousands have surmounted; but turn your thoughts with vigor to some other plan of life, and keep always in your mind, that, with due submission to Providence, a man of genius has been ruined but by himself.* Samuel Johnson

It is probable that Johnson was conscious of the effect of the effect of the repeated "s" sound in the paragraph.

Sometimes alliteration works subconsciously and has a subtle effect. The speaker may not even be aware of the assonance in his speech. However, the writer probably uses it consciously.

Once again, do you hear all the sibilant (hissing "s"

sound) in several words of the following sentence - and not only at the beginning of a word?

> *Somehow, it was hotter then:*
> *A black dog suffered on a summer's day; bony mules hitched to Hoover carts flicked flies in the sweltering shade of the live oaks on the square. Men's stiff collars wilted by nine in the morning. Ladies bathed before noon, after their three o'clock naps, and by nightfall were like soft teacakes with frostings of sweat and sweet talcum.*
> **To kill a Mockingbird**

Alliteration is important not only in literature; in the marketing industry, it makes brand names more interesting.

Best Buy
Coca-Cola
Dunkin' Donuts
Bed Bath & Beyond

Tongue twisters (the very word is alliterative) are often a series of consonants. In this case they are not used for pleasant artistic reason, but rather for the humorous effect of the difficulty of pronunciation.

> *She sells seashells by the seashore.*
> *Peter picked a peck of pickled peppers.*
> *The sinking ship sunk.*

I slit the sheet so I sit on the slit sheet.

Alliteration is so pleasing to the speaker and hearer that many famous phrases, quotes and sayings spring up in most languages. In English the following make use of the repetition of consonants.

Busy as a bee
Dead as a doornail
Get your goat
Give up the ghost
Good as gold
Home sweet home
Last laugh`

Remember the Romans called this Alliteration, and so do we.

All men are mortal....

The Greeks called this Enthymeme.

Sometimes you can make an argument without having it completely logical. You depend on your reader to fill in the blanks in your argument.

This tactic is called an Enthymeme. It is an informally- stated syllogism (a logically progressive argument). The following is a syllogism.

> Starting Point: *All mammals are warm-blooded.*
> Next Point: *All black dogs are mammals.*
> Conclusion: *Therefore, all black dogs are warm- blooded.*

It is possible, and usually very effective, to leave out either one of the steps in the argument or the conclusion to the argument. This is an enthymeme. The omitted part must be clearly understood by the reader. Usually it is the starting point that is omitted:

> *Since we received your application after April 10th, it will not be considered.*
> (Omitted starting point: Only applications submitted before April 10 will be considered.)

He is an American citizen, so he must have democratic principles.
(Omitted starting point: All American citizens have democratic principles.)

An enthymeme can also be written by omitting the minor or following (often the second) point:

Pete is allergic to peanuts, so he cannot eat a Snickers bar. (Omitted following point: Snicker bars contain peanuts.)

A mechanic can be good only when he keeps up with the latest technology. This is why you are not a good mechanic. (Omitted following point: You are not up to date.)

The writer can also omit the conclusion, in cases when the two premises clearly point to it:

My mother never makes a pie without freshly picked apples, and she couldn't get fresh apples this year. (Missing conclusion: She didn't make pies this year.)

Whenever a premise is skipped in an enthymeme, the reader assumes that it is a commonplace and widely accepted generalization. However, at times the skipped premise might not be of common belief by all readers, and the argument is then received as lacking logic and unacceptable, as in the following statements:

You can tell this camera is no good: it's made in China.

He says Jesus was a great moral teacher, so he must be a practicing Christian.

Those girls are from Southern California? They must be either wild or airheads.

To be accepted as a trustworthy writer you should be careful in your own writing to not use this device dishonestly, that is, not to try to pass off or sneak in clearly controversial statements for the omitted premises.

In summary, the enthymeme is a handy logical shorthand, and can be useful in your writing as a way to slightly understate while clearly pointing out some assertion, usually an omitted conclusion.

By making the readers work out the argument for themselves, you get your conclusion across to them, yet in a softer way than by expressing it clearly:

Remember the Greeks called this Enthymeme

Word Sandwich

The Greeks called this Diacope

It is the repetition of a word or phrase after another word or phrase. This is way to gain emphasis is called diacope in literary and rhetorical circles.

Note: Since you have come up to here in this book, we can consider that you are a member of "literary/rhetorical circles". Congratulations!

The term comes from the Greek roots *dia cop*, "cut in two":

You insert a name or a title in the middle of the principal word or phrase. This emphasizes the second word, making it the "last word" on the topic.

Go, girl go!

It's hot, boiling hot!

"All lost! To prayers, to prayers! All lost!"
The Tempest

You're not fully clean until you're Zestfully clean." **Advertising slogan for Zest soap**

"I hate to be poor, and we are degradingly poor, offensively poor, miserably poor, beastly poor." **Charles Dickens, Mutual Friend**

"Of course, in an age of madness, to expect to be untouched by madness is a form of madness. But the pursuit of sanity can be a form of madness, too."
(Saul Bellow, Henderson the Rain King. Viking, 1959)

"I knew it. Born in a hotel room—and goddamn it— died in a hotel room." **Last words of Eugene O'Neill**

You better be careful, I tell you, you better be careful

He will finish it, said his mother; he will finish it.

We give thanks to Thee, 0 God, we give

thanks...
Psalm 75:1

Remember the Greeks called this Diacope

173

The blind man picked up his hammer and saw

The Greeks called this Antiphrasis

∂❧

A figure of speech in which a word or phrase is used in a sense contrary to its normal meaning to achieve an ironic or humorous effect:

> *Yes, I killed him. I killed him for money —*
> *and a woman — and I didn't get the money*
> *and I didn't get the woman. Pretty, isn't it?"*
> **(Double Indemnity, 1944)**

> *"Come here, Tiny," he said to the fat*
> *man.*

> *It was a cool 115 degrees in the*
> *shade.*

> *My youngest daughter is a teenager, a*
> *teenager going on 29.*

If you use this way of expressing yourself well, you can give life to your writing and speaking. It is very useful to inject a little humor into a serious piece without losing the serious tone of the balance of the statement.

It also expresses irony or sarcasm in adversarial or argumentative contexts.

174

You want more money? I'll give you more money.

You ate the fish even though you knew it was three weeks old? Brilliant!

.

Thanks for clapping me on the back when I just broke two ribs. You always do the right thing!

She's only a young lady of 50 years. It is a cool 102 in the shade.

They tell me you wrecked the car. Beautiful! Beautiful!

He's more Catholic than the Pope!

Remember the Greeks called this Antiphrasis

Very Punny!

&

Although you probably won't use puns in your writing, they are included here for three reasons:

1. They were used by many writers such as Shakespeare, Marshall McLuhan, Oscar Wilde, James Joyce, Plautus and many others.
2. They show you good examples of clever understanding and use of words both literally and figuratively
3. They're fun!

The following is largely taken from *Pun, Wikipedia*.

> *The pun is a form of word play that suggests two or more meanings, by exploiting multiple meanings of words, or of similar-sounding words, for an intended humorous or rhetorical effect.*

Puns in-jokes or idiomatic constructions, usually work only with a particular language and most times can't be translated. For example,

176

English: *Camping is intense (in tents)*

French: *Les morts ont les obsèques (les zobs secs)*

Spanish: *No es lo mismo huele a traste, que atrás te huele.*

Puns are used to create humor and sometimes require logic, creativity, and a large vocabulary to appreciate them. An attraction to puns is said to be a sign of intelligence. Puns are an excellent way to progress in learning a foreign language.

Puns can be classified in various ways.

The **homophonic** pun, uses word pairs which <u>sound alike</u> but do not have the same meaning. They are funny when heard

> You can tune a guitar, but you can't tuna fish.
>
> Two silk worms had a race. They ended up in a tie.
>
> I didn't like my beard at first. Then it grew on me.
>
> I stayed up all night to see where the sun went. Then it dawned on me.
>
> Broken pencils are pointless.
>
> What do you call a dinosaur with a big vocabulary? A thesaurus.
>
> I paid two dollars for Velcro. What a rip-off!

A **homographic** pun depends on words which are spelled the same have different meanings and sounds. They are understood and appreciated as clever when they are read, not when they are heard, contrary to homophonic puns.

> *I failed communism class because of lousy Marx.*
>
> *I got a job at a bakery because I needed dough.*
>
> *Atheism is a non-prophet institution.*
>
> *Jokes about German sausage are the wurst.*
>
> *How does Moses make tea? Hebrews it.*
>
> *A dyslexic man walks into a bra.*
>
> *When you get a bladder infection, urine trouble.*
>
> *All the toilets in the police station have been stolen. Now the police have nothing to go on.*
>
> *Haunted French pancakes give me the crepes.*

Like other forms of wordplay, puns are occasionally used for their attention-getting qualities, making it common in titles and the names of places, characters, and organizations, and in advertising and slogans.

I buy my ties at the "Tiecoon Tie Shop."

You can buy the best chicken in town at the "Pullet Surprise."

You get the best booze at the "Planet of the Grapes Wine Shop."

"Let your fingers do the walking" **The Yellow Pages** "

We answer to a higher authority". **Hebrew National Salami**

Here are some corporate slogans that play on words.

"Enjoyed for centuries straight" **Wyborowa Vodka**
"Technology the world calls on" **Northern Telecom**
"When it rains, it pours!" **Morton Salt**
"Picks up where your dog leaves off" **Pooper Scooper**

Finally, here is an extensive list of puns which I don't know how to classify:

1.. The fattest knight at King Arthur's round table was Sir Cumference. He got fat from too much pi.

2.. I thought I saw an eye doctor on an Alaskan island, but it turned out to be an optical Aleutian.

3.. She was only a whiskey maker, but he loved her still.

4.. A rubber band pistol was confiscated from algebra class, because it was a weapon of math disruption.

5.. No matter how much you push the envelope, it'll still be stationery.

6.. A dog gave birth to puppies near the road and was cited for littering.

7.. A grenade thrown into a kitchen in France would result in Linoleum Blownapart

9.. A hole has been found in the nudist camp wall. The police are looking into it.

12. Two hats were hanging on a hat rack in the hallway. One hat said to the other: 'You stay here; I'll go on a head.'

13. I wondered why the baseball kept getting bigger. Then it hit me.

14. A sign on the lawn at a drug rehab center said: "Keep off the Grass".'

15. The 5 foot 2 fortune-teller who escaped from prison was a small medium at large.

16. The soldier who survived mustard gas and pepper spray is now a seasoned veteran.

17. A backward poet writes inverse.

18. In a democracy it's your vote that counts. In feudalism it's your count that votes.

19. When cannibals ate a missionary, they got a taste of religion.

20. If you jumped off the bridge in Paris, you'd be in Seine .

21. A vulture boards an airplane, carrying two dead raccoons. The stewardess looks at him and says, "I'm sorry, sir, only one carrion allowed per passenger".

22. Two fish swim into a concrete wall. One turns to the other and says "Dam!"

23. Two Eskimos sitting in a kayak were chilly, so they lit a fire in the craft. Unsurprisingly it sank, proving once again that you can't have your kayak and heat it too.

24. Two hydrogen atoms meet. One says, "I've lost my electron." The other says "Are you sure?' The first replies, "Yes, I'm positive."

25. Did you hear about the Buddhist who refused Novocain during a root canal? His goal: transcend dental medication.

27. A hangover is the wrath of grapes.

28. Without geometry, life is pointless.

28. Reading while sunbathing makes you well-red.

29. I tried to catch some fog, but I mist.

30. I changed my smart phone's name to Titanic. It's syncing now.

Here's a few more:

When chemists die, they barium.

I know a guy who's addicted to brake fluid, but he says he can stop any time.

I'm reading a book on anti-gravity, and I can't put it down.

I did a show about puns; it was a play on words. They told me I had Type-A blood, but it was a Typo.

Why were the aboriginals here first? They had reservations.

Class trip to the Coca-Cola factory, but no pop quiz.

The Energizer bunny was arrested and charged with battery.

Did you hear about the cross-eyed teacher who lost her job because she couldn't control her pupils?

What does a hungry clock do? It goes back 4 seconds.

I wondered why the baseball was getting bigger. Then it hit me!

England has no kidney bank, but it does have a Liverpool.

I used to be a banker, but then I lost interest.

I used to think I was indecisive, but now I'm not so sure

Remember the Greeks called it
Paronomasia But we call them CORNY!

EPILOGUE

Surely you found some ideas for your writing in this little book. To use them to wake up your writing is good; to use them too much is not good.

The ideal is for you to keep your writing lively by using the proper rhetorical device according to your need to emphasize or clarify; organize or arrange; or embellish or display your writing style.

It will rarely be possible or good for you to set out to use one of these ways of expression just for the sake of using it. They will be more effective when they sprout naturally as you write.

To reach this flowering in your writing you need to practice identifying the use of rhetorical devices in good writing, and then practice using, never abusing, them yourself.

Get a piece of paper or open a file in your computer to meet the challenge of writing an appropriate phrase for each the devices mentioned in this book.

This exercise is a little forced so you may have trouble composing a response to the challenge. But do your best. At the end of the challenges, you will find the names of the devices in the same order as the challenges.

See if you can write phrases that **emphasize and clarify** a thought, for example, you can:

1. Provide additional information to a phrase.
2. Stop one thought and jump to another.
3. Compare different things.
4. Present something in a positive light.
5. Emphasize a thought by denying it.
6. Express doubt about something, then defend it.
7. Repeat a word after interrupting the flow of a phrase.
8. Make an difference between ideas clearer.
9. Refer to a famous person.
10. Ask a question you know the answer to.
11. Give an example to support your thought.
12. Exaggerate a description.
13. Ask a question, then answer it.
14. Deny the opposite of the main idea.
15. Take back a thought, then state it differently.
16. Repeat the same idea differently.
17. Use a proverb, or wise saying to support your idea.
18. Understate an idea as less than it really is.

Try to write a few words that will **organize and arrange** your content, for example, you can:

1. Write a few thoughts with no connectors (and, but, etc.).

2. Express the contrast between two ideas.

3. Write using the same word or phrase at the beginning and end of a series, with a different word in between them, in the following pattern: word 1, word 2; word 2, word 1.

4. Balance the first part of a grammatical construction with the second part, changing the order of the parts.

5. Present ideas in order of importance.

6. Begin and end phrase with the same word.

7. Change the order of words.

8. Balance words and phrases equally.

9. Write successive clauses with or without punctuation.

10. Insert new or explanatory phrase.

11. Use many connecting words.

12. Interrupt a phrases's flow with new idea.

13. Link similar words or expressions.

Write something in a **flashy attention getting style**, for example, you can:

1. Repeat the same consonant sound.
2. Refer to a well-known thing or event.
3. Start successive phrases with the same beginning.
4. Use a word as a different part of speech.
5. Use a word in unusual manner.
6. Call out to a person or thing.
7. Repeat the same vowel sound.
8. Use words in an unusual way.
9. Repeat the same word at the end of successive sentences.
10. Make reference to a well-known person.
11. Make the point that one thing IS another.
12. Use the name of one thing to refer to another.
13. Write a phrase that contradicts itself.
14. Refer to a thing or animal as human.
15. Anticipate a counter argument.
16. Repeat the same idea with different words.
17. Make a word play using similar meanings and sounds.
18. Refer to a thing as "like" or "as" another.
19. Make a part stand for the whole or the whole for a part.

Go back and check if you got the idea and were able to use the rhetorical device correctly. The challenges referred to these devices.

EMPHASIS AND CLARIFICATION
1. Amplificatio
2. Anacoluthon
3. Analogy
4. Antanagoge
5. Apophasis
6. Aporia
7. Diacope
8. Distinctio
9. Eponym
10. Erotesis
11. Exemplum
12. Hyperbole
13. Hypophora
14. Litotes
15. Metanoia
16. Scesis Onomaton
17. Sententia
18. Understatement

Go back and check if you got the idea and were able to use the rhetorical device correctly. The challenges referred to these devices.

ORGANIZATION AND ARRANCGEMENT

1. Asyndeton
2. Antithesis
3. Antimetabole
4. Chiasmus
5. Climax
6. Epanalepsis
7. Hyperbaton
8. Parallelism
9. Parataxis
10. Parenthesis
11. Polysyndeton
12. Sentential Adverb
13. Zeugma

Go back and check if you got the idea and were able to use the rhetorical device correctly. The challenges referred to these devices.

STYLE AND DISPLAY

1. Alliteration
2. Allusion
3. Anaphora
4. Anthimeria
5. Antiphrasis
6. Apostrophe
7. Assonance
8. Catachresis
9. Epistrophe
10. Eponym
11. Metaphor
12. Metonymy
13. Oxymoron
14. Personification
15. Procatalepsis
16. Pleonasm
17. Paronomasia
18. Simile
19. Synecdoche

INDEX

**If you liked this book, please rate it favorably
by clicking on**:

https://tinyurl.com/y98dh3xp

;

OUR BOOKS

Please always give us a review on Amazon

ESL and Adult Learners of English
CAN WRITE WELL

Writing for advanced ESL (English as Second Language) readers and other interested adult learners. An exploration of the Grammar, Spelling, Usage, as well as a Method that will give them information, skills, and confidence. The book contains extensive cross referencing among related topics. Most of the chapters have exercises and answers.

- PRINT:
  Spain and the EU: http://tinyurl.com/oc6cwbg
  United States: http://tinyurl.com/ncyufe7
- DIGITAL Worldwide:
  http://4.guacuru2.pay.clickbank.net

- Amazon Kindle: https://tinyurl.com/ya3qhq8p

If you purchase this book on Amazon, please give it a good review! THANKS!

Escucha y Habla inglés,
Claves de Pronunciación
y Gramática para el hispano

Cuesta más la recta final. Este libro ayudará al hispano que ya sabe algo de inglés y que quiere llegar a dominar el idioma aún más. Es fruto de la experiencia de muchos años de enseñanza a inmigrantes hispanos en el sistema CUNY (Universidad de la Ciudad de Nueva York y en universidades privadas y estatales de Bolivia y Perú. ¡Escucha y Habla Inglés! ofrece "claves" para evitar los errores de gramática y pronunciación que asechan al hispano.

Consíguelo en Amazon, en forma impresa o la versión Kindle:
http://tinyurl.com/jmyx5xw
Recommend this book to your friends.

Wake up your Writing

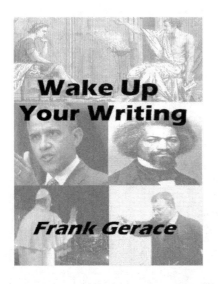

A light hearted look at the classical rhetorical devices aimed at providing inspiration and models to new writers. Examples are given of everyday English, classical and modern writers.

Get it from Amazon in print or as Kindle: https://tinyurl.com/yc9wlqjw

If you purchase this book on Amazon, please give it a good review! THANKS!

THE WRITE ENGLISH BETTER SERIES

Number 1

THE CRAZY VERBS OF ENGLISH
Whaaa? Phrasals and Gerunds?
Go TO: https://www.amazon.com/ebook/dp/4HF8PLM

Number 2

I SHOT A BEAR IN MY PAJAMAS
Common errors the Adult Learner Makes Writing English
Go TO: https://www.amazon.com/ebook/dp/00FNB1BFE

Number 3

ROSES ARE RED AND CHILI IS HOT
Use adjectives better, and get started writing
Go TO: https://www.amazon.com/ebook/dp/B079Y9ZZ9H

Number 4

LIFE IS LIKE BOX OF CHOCOLATE
Put Punch in Your Writing with Similes and Metaphors
Go TO: https://www.amazon.com/ebook/dp/B07BR63L8Y

Number 5

I REALLY MEAN IT
Learn how to emphasize and clarify your writing
Go TO:
https://www.amazon.com/ebook/dp/B07BR964WN

Number 6

JUST LIKE THE RAILROAD RAILS
Use PARALLELISM in your writing
Go TO: https://www.amazon.com/ebook/dp/B07C9GNS9F

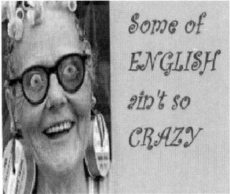

SOME OF ENGLISH AIN'T SO CRAZY
Find the sense in English Spelling and Irregular Verbs!
Go TO: https://www.amazon.com/ebook/dp/B07BR7FJM8

Number 8

THE HIP BONE'S CONNECTED TO...
Fix run-on and other sentence errors with connectors
Go TO:
https://www.amazon.com/ebook/dp/B07BRC3MSX

Number 9

GET YOUR ACT TOGETHER
Organize your writing with useful tricks
Go TO:
https://www.amazon.com/ebook/dp/B07BTJMTZT

Number 10

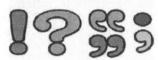

DOT YOUR I'S
Use Capitalization and Punctuation correctly
Go TO:
https://www.amazon.com/ebook/dp/B07BTPMDKX

Number 11

FLAUNT IT!
Write with expressions that show style and display
Go TO:
https://www.amazon.com/ebook/dp/B07CB28D2G

Number 12

USE CLUES TO LEARN VOCABULARY
Exercises and Answers to learn without dictionary
Go TO:
https://www.amazon.com/ebook/dp/B07BX6WS89

Number 13

SPELLING
Important and not impossible
Go TO:
https://www.amazon.com/ebook/dp/B07BY76NVX

Number 14

VERBS
Exercises and Answers for your writing
Go TO:
https://www.amazon.com/ebook/dp/B07BYGXLFX

Number 15

Parts of Speech are

Different Flavors of
WORDS

PARTS OF SPEECH
Improve your writing
Go TO:
https://www.amazon.com/ebook/dp/B07BZQXYTV

Number 16

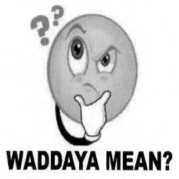

WADDAYA MEAN?

WADDAYA MEAN?
Write to get our point across!
Go TO:
https://www.amazon.com/ebook/dp/B07CBNCLRG

WRITE THAT REPORT!
A Simple Way to Get Started
Go TO:
https://www.amazon.com/ebook/dp/B07C2LX5M5

Number 18

Apples & Oranges

Use Comparisons and
Differences in your
WRITING

Comparisons and Differences
Go TO:
https://www.amazon.com/ebook/dp/B07C2LXRQC

Good Sentences

make

Strong Paragraphs

The Bricks and Walls of Your Thought Building
Go TO:
https://www.amazon.com/ebook/dp/B07C45JCC1

We call them names, we shout out their names, we describe them
Go TO:
https://www.amazon.com/ebook/dp/B07BZQXYTV

TRY TO LIGHT
THE FIRE

THE SINKING SHIP
SUNK

Listen to Your Words
Go TO:
https://www.amazon.com/ebook/dp/B07C6MT6NX

The Leer Es Poder Series

MUESTRA ILUSTRATIVA

Claves de Gramática y Pronunciación
para hispanoparlantes
Go TO:
https://www.amazon.com/ebook/dp/B00FNB1BFE

LA COMUNICACIÓN SOCIAL
en América Latina de 1973 a 2005

Go TO: https://www.amazon.com/ebook/dp/B009TIJLBI

Other Recommendations:

1. http://www.GoodAccent.com
   A collection of online resources to help
   learners of English achieve a good North
   American English accent in their speech.

2. http://www.EscuchaHabla.com/
   Escucha y habla Inglés: Claves de Gramática y
   Pronunciación del Inglés para el hispano.

3. http://www.InglesParaLatinos.com
   Un sitio de múltiples páginas con ayuda para
   la lectura, ortografía, pronunciación, escritura
   del Inglés.

4. http://www.BooksLibros.com/LibrosEnEspano
   l.php
   Libros de todo tipo y de todo precio en
   español. Buy books in Spanish and about
   Spanish. Also find books in English.

5. http://www.BooksLibros.com/SpanishForNino
   s.htm
   Experiences and tips from parents on Spanish
   for your kids.

Made in the USA
Lexington, KY
07 August 2019